PREACHING THE
RESURRECTION

Twenty-two Great Easter Sermons

Edited by
ALTON M. MOTTER

MUHLENBERG PRESS
Philadelphia

© 1959 by Muhlenberg Press

The Library of Congress has catalogued this book as follows:

Motter, Alton M ed. Preaching the Resurrection; twenty-two great Easter sermons. Philadelphia, Muhlenberg Press, 1959. 189 p. 19 cm. 1. Easter —Sermons. 2. Sermons, American. I. Title
BV4259.M63   252.6   59-7237 ‡

Printed in U.S.A.   UB

This book is affectionately dedicated to those Christian personalities whose influence in my life, in this 25th year of ministry, has been such that—though they no longer live in the flesh—they continue to bear witness to so high a quality of life and discipleship that they can never die.

Alton M. Motter

PREFACE

What should Easter mean to Christians now living past the midway point of the Twentieth Century? Such was the question put to twenty-two of America's Christian leaders. This book contains their replies.

The contributors hold various positions of Christian responsibility. Nearly one-half are pastors of congregations. An equal number are theological teachers. Two are college presidents. Two are bishops. Collectively, they come from the six largest Protestant church families in America.

These men deal with varied segments of the Easter theme. There is new light here and new power. Some speak more directly to our spiritual condition than others. But all have something to say about Jesus Christ and the power of his resurrection for Twentieth Century Christians.

This volume was produced with the belief that it will make a valuable contribution to the thinking and devotional life of both laymen and clergymen about the deeper meaning of Christianity's greatest day. To the extent that it does this and provides added illumination for life's common pilgrimage, its mission will have been fulfilled.

ALTON M. MOTTER

Denver, Colorado
January, 1959

CONTENTS

1. THE GOSPEL OF LIFE
   Conrad Bergendoff   1

2. THE ASSURANCES OF EASTER
   Edgar M. Carlson   10

3. LIVING BEFORE WE DIE
   Edwin T. Dahlberg   16

4. THE LIVING CHRIST
   O. A. Geiseman   22

5. OUT OF THIS WORLD
   J. Wallace Hamilton   30

6. THE EASTER MESSAGE
   Martin J. Heinecken   42

7. THE CHRIST EVENT
   Elmer G. Homrighausen   57

8. SOMNOLENT SAINTS
   William H. Hudnut, Jr.   68

9. CAN WE BELIEVE IN ETERNAL LIFE?
   William E. Hulme   75

10. THE QUESTION, THE CANDLE, THE ARROW
    Gerald Kennedy   82

11. WORDS OF THE RISEN LORD
    A. R. Kretzmann   90

12. CHRIST BREAKS THROUGH
    David A. MacLennan   99

13 THE DAY OF THE EARTHQUAKE
Roy Pearson 107

14 WHAT DIFFERENCE DOES EASTER MAKE?
James A. Pike 116

15 THE UNSEEN EASTER
Liston Pope 128

16 THE GLADNESS OF GOD
David H. C. Read 135

17 GOD'S GREAT NEVERTHELESS
Paul E. Scherer 142

18 THE IMPACT OF THE RESURRECTION
Frederick W. Schroeder 152

19 FESTUS
Joseph Sittler, Jr. 159

20 TOO GREAT FOR THE GRAVE
Ralph W. Sockman 165

21 THE POWER OF HIS RESURRECTION
Dwight E. Stevenson 173

22 WHEN LIFE IS THE CLIMAX OF DEATH
Morris Wee 180

1

THE GOSPEL OF LIFE

by CONRAD BERGENDOFF

President, Augustana College, Rock Island, Illinois

"He is not God of the dead, but of the living."
—MATTHEW 22:32

TAKEN by itself the resurrection of Christ, or any resurrection, is incredible. No wonder that the disciples were met by ridicule and unbelief when they proclaimed their Lord risen from the dead. It is the reaction of all ages to an announcement of something contrary to experience and evidently opposed to all that reason can make out of life. "Paul, you are mad," said Festus the governor, when Paul affirmed before him and King Agrippa that "Christ was the first to rise from the dead." "Your great learning is turning you mad," was the opinion of the governor, showing that he did not think Paul's proclamation was due to ignorance.

But the resurrection is not an isolated fact. It cannot be taken by itself. It is a mountain peak in the history of humanity, but a peak that rises gradually from a great base. It is part of a range whose summit is surrounded by a whole series of related heights. Indeed, to those who first proclaimed the resurrection this event was the culminating point of the history of humanity.

When the disciples began to witness to the resurrection before the crowds and authorities in Jerusalem, they asserted simply, "The God of our fathers raised Jesus whom you killed by hanging him on a tree." But in the few words "The God of our fathers" lay a whole religion, and the resurrection of Jesus Christ cannot be understood apart from the "God of our fathers."

Here is where Stephen started, when he testified of his faith in Christ whom he saw "standing at the right hand of God." "Brethren and fathers," he said, "hear me." Then he began with the story of the appearance of "the God of glory" to Abraham, bidding him to leave Mesopotamia for a "land which I will show you." He traced the whole history of Israel, through Moses and David and Solomon. To this people had come the law, the temple, the prophets. But they received neither prophets nor, finally, the "Righteous One," and the judgment of God was upon them for not beholding the revelation of God. Among those who participated in the stoning of this early witness to the resurrection of Jesus was a man named Saul.

The story of the resurrection comes at the very end of the gospels, and the gospels follow the whole of the Old Testament. To break into the meaning of a story or of a play when it is half way through is to miss the connection of parts and often to miss the meaning of the whole. The Easter worshiper who knows nothing of the parts of the church year which have gone before can catch very little in the drama of the divine action. For Advent and Lent come first. The appearance of the Risen One has little meaning to those who come merely to gape and to gossip. One of his very first appearances was to two men who were much disturbed by what had happened. They knew the background, but even for them Jesus found it necessary to interpret "in all the scriptures the things concerning himself, beginning with Moses and all the prophets." The road to the open tomb runs only through the holy land of Scripture.

CONRAD BERGENDOFF

The context of the resurrection of Christ is an Old and New Testament whose entire theme is the creation of light and life out of darkness and death. The opening word of the God whom this book reveals is, "Let there be light." It is a book of miracles from beginning to end. And is the initial miracle the least? No human mind can comprehend the creation of light, or recall the circumstances when what had been chaos and void took form. We exalt our feeble reason by our formula of $E = MC^2$ and think we are on the path to discovery of truth, but

"Where were you when I laid the foundation of the earth?
Tell me, if you have understanding.
Who determined its measurements—surely you know!
Or who stretched the line upon it?
On what were its bases sunk,
Or who laid its cornerstone,
When the morning stars sang together,
And all the sons of God shouted for joy?" (Job 38:4-7).

Aeons are compressed in the opening chapter of Genesis. The whole sweep of the universe is contained in the simple sentences that tell of the ordering of the universe and the coming of life. We can as little explain the movement of the stars as the movement of the forces making for human life. Nor does this book pretend to give explanations. Its proclamation is single and unique. God did it. He created heavens and earth. He gave man life. Out of an infinite tomb of nothingness he called forth the principle of living beings. The God who raised Christ from the dead was the God who called forth every living thing. Easter dawn reflects a light that dawned first on Creation's morn.

Sometimes people are surprised that this is not the main

emphasis of Scripture. It is not forgotten. It is always in the background. But the central theme of the Bible is the creation, not of the universe, but of a people. It was of Abraham, Moses, David, that Stephen spoke in the defense of his faith. In the book of Psalms some of the longest compositions are Psalms 103 to 107. Read them carefully and you will see that they are summaries of Israel's history, celebrating God's great acts in shaping a people of his own. The marvelous escape at the Red Sea is a recurring note. They do stress what we have already mentioned:

"When thou sendest forth thy Spirit, they are created;
And thou renewest the face of the ground"

but the greater space is given to:

"The covenant which he made with Abraham,
His sworn promise to Isaac
Which he confirmed to Jacob as a statute,
To Israel as an everlasting covenant."

This, too, is the theme of the prophets. They realized the unfaithfulness of Israel, but proclaimed a faithfulness of God which defied human reason. God's purpose was not to fail, however undependable man might be. Indeed, the power of God to achieve his purpose in creating a people that would know him and turn away from the idols of the nations is guaranteed by the power that is his to uphold the created universe. When the prophet Isaiah feels that the iniquity of his people is past redemption, he is reminded,

"Why do you say, O Jacob,
And speak, O Israel,
'My way is hid from the Lord
And my right is disregarded by my God?'
Have you not known?

Have you not heard?
The Lord is the everlasting God,
The Creator of the ends of the earth.
He does not faint or grow weary.
His understanding is unsearchable."

This, too, was the conclusion of Paul, centuries later, when he looked back on the course of God's redemption. For it was not through the worldly power of Israel that God would achieve his goal. That power was shattered. Yet through a remnant he kept alive the hope of a holy kingdom, and in the fulness of time he himself came into human life in order to create among them a new spirit. That he should not be accepted by those who called themselves by his name is the supreme tragedy of human history. But it was his will to create faith wherever men would hear the news of the kingdom. Rejected by Israel, he formed a new Israel, and perpetuated his covenant of mercy and life. This was the marvelous way of God which evoked the cry of Paul, "O the depth of the riches and wisdom and knowledge of God! How unsearchable are his judgments and how inscrutable his ways!"

The resurrection of Christ is but one phase of the miraculous ministry of Christ, which involved the resurrection of a people. He came to a world dead in sin, without hope, and blinded by pride and greed. He came to rekindle a spark of a promise which had been the charter of the original Israel, but he came with a message which now was to reach all nations. It was a message of life where death prevailed.

The writer of the fourth gospel beheld in Jesus the dawn of a second day of creation. "In him was life, and the life was the light of men. The light shines in the darkness, and the darkness has not overcome it . . . to all who

THE GOSPEL OF LIFE

received him, who believed in his name, he gave power to become the children of God." Here was a new beginning. Those "born of God" were created in an image of grace and truth—"and from his fulness have we all received, grace upon grace."

The gospels are the story of this creative light as it moved from Bethlehem to Golgotha. Unearthly as it was in its purity and power, it was not unrelated to the light that had led the people of the Old Testament on through doubt and despair. It is a light that some had beheld in faith, but now was closer to man than ever before. "We have beheld his glory, glory as of the only Son from the Father," was the confession of John. Another disciple could write, "For it is the God who said, 'Let light shine out of darkness,' who has shone in our hearts to give the light of the knowledge of the glory of God in the face of Christ."

He himself was aware that his light was not his own, but "reflects the glory of God and bears the very stamp of his nature, upholding the universe by his word of power." He spoke of his relationship to the Father in a way that seemed blasphemous to his critics. But everywhere he emphasized that he was sent of the Father, he came from the Father, he spoke what the Father gave him to say. It is a relationship that transcends human reason, for it is unique. The closest man has come to describe it is to call him the Son of God. He could say, "I and the Father are one" and claim that from the Father he had power to "lay down my life of my own accord, and power to take it again."

In all his ministry and his words there is no fear of death. The author of the epistle to the Hebrews described Christ's mission thus: "to destroy him who has the power of death, that is, the devil, and deliver all those who through fear of death were subject to lifelong bondage." Certainly there was no fear of death in him, and his word to his people was not to fear. He saw his task in the prophetic passage, "to preach good news to the poor . . . to proclaim release to the captives . . . to set at liberty those who are oppressed." To Martha, who had expressed belief in "resurrection at the last day," Jesus said, "I am the resurrection and the life; he who believes in me, though he die, yet shall he live, and whoever lives and believes in me shall never die." His words inspired life in those who heard, and created new strength and hope in body and soul.

To speak of the resurrection of Jesus as if it were a very unexpected event in a life that would be complete without it is to have missed the essential significance of his ministry. His mission was to proclaim the victory of life over death. When Sadducees "who say that there is no resurrection" tried to ridicule the notion of a life after death, he replied, "You are wrong, because you know neither the scriptures nor the power of God . . . have you not read what was said to you by God, 'I am the God of Abraham, and the God of Isaac, and the God of Jacob'? He is not God of the dead, but of the living."

To believe in God is to believe in life. In revealing the glory of God, Jesus Christ revealed the power of life over death, the triumph of light and love and mercy over darkness and hate and anger. To deny the resurrection is to assert the victory of death over life, the failure of humanity as a creation of God, the final night of nothingness over any purpose of a God as known in Christ. "If Christ has not been raised, your faith is futile and you are still in your sins." Not only is our faith futile, but life is futile. If Christ be not raised then the New Testament is a "misrepresentation," and the Old Testament has no meaning beside that of a disillusionment. Then life has no explanation, and the universe is a meaningless accident.

But those who so deny the miracle of the resurrection "know neither the scriptures nor the power of God." For Scripture is the revelation of miracles from beginning to end and the gospel "is the power of God for salvation to every one who has faith." The story of the resurrection is no more incomprehensible than the story of human life itself. It is a miracle, because the thoughts of God are beyond our thoughts, but not on that account untrue. "For we did not follow cleverly devised myths when we made known unto you the power and coming of our Lord Jesus Christ, but we were eyewitnesses of his majesty," declared one of those eyewitnesses. Jesus Christ arose from the dead because death had no power over him. Death cannot ultimately overcome life. The final fact is life, not death. The creation of the universe, the creation of a people, these are themselves victories over nothingness. The God whose very name is "I Am" is the guarantee that we live. Because Christ lives, those in Christ shall live.

Such is the message of the church of Christ. The church is the new Israel, the people of the new covenant. Through it God realizes the eternal purpose declared to Abraham. In it the Spirit of him who raised up Jesus from the dead gives life even now to mortal bodies and "makes us sit with him in the heavenly places in Christ Jesus, that in the coming ages he might show the immeasurable riches of his grace in kindness toward us in Christ Jesus."

The opening chapters of the Bible picture the creation of light and the forming of man.

The closing book pictures the new people of God in the new heavens and the new earth. "And they sang a new song, saying,

Worthy art thou to take the scroll and to open its

seals, for thou wast slain and by the blood didst ransom men for God
From every tribe and tongue and people and nation and hast made them a kingdom and priests to our God and they shall reign on earth."

In the context of the Book of Life the resurrection of Christ is no isolated fact, no interpolation of a generation that knew less than the eyewitnesses. It is the key to the whole drama of salvation. Wherever you touch the veins of Scripture you feel the heartbeat of the resurrection. The Old Testament makes it necessary; the New Testament shows its consequences. Far from being a figment of someone's imagination, it is the creative fact which makes the old new, and which conquers death and fulfils the purpose of God in creation. Only the resurrected Christ is worthy to unroll the scrolls of humanity's history and to provide reason for the existence of the universe.

2

THE ASSURANCES OF EASTER

by EDGAR M. CARLSON

President, Gustavus Adolphus College, St. Peter, Minnesota

MATTHEW 28:1-8

SINCE "it began to dawn" on this Easter Day the sidewalks and streets and highways around the world have been echoing with the sound of worshipers on their way to join in the fellowship of those who gather around a mysterious empty tomb. From it they seek some good answer about the riddle of life and death. Some of them, no doubt, are merely caught up in the excitement of a holiday season that still retains the character of a "holy day." But most of them, I think, are prompted by some inner longing, more or less definite, for a hope that shall transcend the fate of death. They think they may find it in the message of a resurrection.

"As it began to dawn" on that first Easter morning, the streets were still except for the almost silent movement of the women who had been last at the Cross—on their way to be first at the tomb. They were on an errand of love; they would complete the anointing of their dear friend, whose life had been interrupted by the sunset of that long and awful Friday on which they had lost him. And their hearts were heavy still. They had seen a dream shattered, a hope disappointed, a promise unfulfilled. He to whom they had given their loyalty and allegiance and affection as the Messiah who was to redeem Israel had been done to death at the hands of brutal and heartless men. The gaunt crosses still stood upon the hill to mock them, and to mock the hopes of all humanity as well.

The Sabbath day had passed wearily and a dull dread of an uncertain but gloomy future had settled upon them. They knew not where the road might lead them after what had happened; they only knew that this must still be done —the anointing of the dead must be finished. One might have expected that the stone which they had themselves seen rolled against the door of the tomb would have kept them back, for surely the strength was not in them to roll away the stone. But it is like love not to take seriously into account the obvious reasons for not doing what must be done. They loved him so!

There could not have been one ray of hope in the clouds which hung over them that dawn. The tragedy of Good Friday was too complete. They did not make the journey on the chance that there might still be some hope for another outcome. They knew that he was dead and all was over. Even when they found the stone rolled away and the tomb empty, the only explanation that occurred to them was that someone—his enemies—had stolen away the body and robbed them of that last frail satisfaction of knowing where he lay.

But the angel in gleaming light had another answer. "He is not here, he is risen." And as the meaning of the angel's message came home to them, and later to the disciples, verified and made more real by his appearances among them, the empty tomb became the spur to their unconquerable spirits, the very rock on which their faith could rest, the foundation of their certainty and their fearlessness as they faced tomorrow. He who had been crucified on Good Friday had been "powerfully declared to be the Son of God by the resurrection from the dead."

THE ASSURANCES OF EASTER

They remembered what he had said and they saw new meaning in it. "I am the resurrection and the life; he who believes in me, though he die, yet shall he live." "Because I live, you will live also."

That which happened on that Easter morning is the only adequate cause for the multitudes gathering for worship this morning. In this event and in its meaning for the nations and the centuries, we think we may find a "hope that shall not be put to shame."

I should like to point you to the assurances, the certainties, the securities, that come to us on Easter morning.

First, there is *the assurance that death is not sovereign*. Who has not wondered about it, as he stood beside the earthly remains of a loved one, or perhaps himself faced the prospect of his own death? The race between life and death is always close. In the end, it will be exactly even. All who enter into life by the gateway of birth must leave it by the gateway of death, except as they that are alive at his coming may be spared the experience of death. We may lengthen the life span, we may diminish pain during the years of waiting, we make make life fuller and richer —but in the end, is it not death that wins? This is the final frustration, the final defeat. This is the place where all the controls of life go out of our hands. Here the freedom to choose alternatives comes to an end.

Death carries with it a certain fearful expectation, too, for thoughtful men, for death is the place where we move into the hands of God. We are at his mercy there. There is enough of the image of God in all men to suspect at least, that at this point our destiny rests in his hands. In this life we may ignore him, or scorn him. We may act as though he existed only with our permission; as though we could somehow nullify his existence by not believing in him. But there, at the place of death, if there be any God, our existence and our future depend upon his will and power. We move toward that inevitable encounter with unclean hands and impure hearts. This is "the sting of death."

But if Easter be true, death is not sovereign. To be sure, the faith that life could endure beyond did not originate on Easter morning. "If a man die, shall he live again?" is an ancient question, and it has been answered affirmatively by others. "I know that my redeemer liveth" is a quotation from the Old Testament. Yet, there is something new that came to mankind through the resurrection of Jesus Christ. Early in the church they began to sing, "Not Christ, but death died yesternight." And what was new in the assurance that came to Christians in the face of death was that what lies beyond death and the resurrection is the dominion of this Christ whom they had known and loved. He who had been crucified had risen again and was now the Lord of both the living and the dead. "Pillow my head on no guess when I die." Indeed, there is no guesswork about it any more.

Second, there is *the assurance that God's love is the most certain thing in the world.* The resurrection is not merely a way of getting Jesus back from the dead so he can return to the Father's house. It is itself a part of the revelation of God's love, of his atoning deed, and of his triumph against all foes.

The Cross means much more than any of us can tell; certainly much more than can be told this morning. But at least a part of its meaning, and perhaps the core of it, is this: on the Cross, God was meeting the world's evil, sin and guilt, and bearing it in forgiving love. He could speak the words of forgiveness even from a Cross. Here is the place where men are doing their worst to God, and here is the place where God is doing his best for men.

THE ASSURANCES OF EASTER

He who should have been raised to a throne and offered devotion and praise, was raised on a Cross to die. When it was all over, no one could have raised a voice in protest if he had returned with the fires of judgment. With the evidence against men all in, five scars bearing eternal witness against them and all their pretensions to wisdom and goodness and justice, who could have pleaded for a second chance? But he came back to offer them the same gospel of forgiveness, and asking no more than that men accept it. He sent out his disciples to preach "the remission of sins."

This is the absolute which has entered our faith. You can build on that boundless love of God. Nothing that we can do can change God's love into hatred, for there is nothing that men can do to God which was not done to him when they nailed him to the tree. If we are to be lost, we must be lost against a love like that. And just because it is so free and full, we can be lost. Salvation will never be forced upon us. "But to all who received him, who believed in his name, he gave power to become children of God."

And finally, there is *the assurance that in the end the victory belongs to God*. Sometimes all of us must wonder how it is going to turn out. Evil flaunting itself in the face of righteousness, and good so frail! Our personal lives with their triumphs, about which we prate so much, and their great failures about which we speak so little! And our world with its pretension and its pride! What chance does a kingdom of love have in the midst of it all? Have no fear! God will win. His is the last word, whether it be the word of life or of judgment. The forces in the world that are against him are not his equal. At the place of death, if not before, they all lay down their cheap and shoddy crowns, and only the King of kings remains.

And at the end of it all, is the last chapter of human history to be war and famine, pestilence, devastation and defeat? Is the A-bomb, the H-bomb, or the C-bomb to determine the ultimate fate of our world? Are these stronger than God, in the end? Easter has an answer for it. Here death is turned to life; hope is born out of a Cross. This is the nature of God, to take the tragedy of life and of the world and to turn it into life and hope. If it should be that the world is to be vaporized into mushroom clouds of destruction—and we know now how it could happen—then he will turn those clouds of destruction into the clouds of his glory. The world's passing will be his coming again "on the clouds of glory."

These are the assurances of Easter. We need not fear. Christ is risen, indeed!

3

LIVING BEFORE WE DIE

by EDWIN T. DAHLBERG

Pastor, Delmar Baptist Church, St. Louis, Missouri, and President, National Council of the Churches of Christ in the United States of America

"I came that they may have life, and have it abundantly."

—JOHN 10:10

ONE beautiful Sunday morning in July, 1955, I preached at the Church of the Open Air, a drive-in theater on the shores of Gull Lake in northern Minnesota. Surrounded on three sides by the forest trees, the Church of the Open Air is bordered on the fourth side by the shining waters of the lake. Every Sunday it attracts a thousand people or more, who through the years have listened to the inspired preaching of Dr. Howard A. Vernon, the founder of this great open air church. The advertising slogan of the church is, "Come as you are—Stay in your car."

The service the morning we were there was packed with drama. The Sunday preceding, Dr. Vernon had preached a stirring sermon on the subject I have chosen for this sermon. A profound thinker, he stated clearly his faith in life after death. "But," said he, "most of us do not give enough attention to life *before* death. Our hymns and our sermons are centered so much on the life hereafter that we become other-worldly, forgetting Jesus' emphasis on the life here and now. We must remember that God is not a

God of the dead but of the living. He came in order that we might have abundant life today."

His whole emphasis made a profound impression on us all. Hence it was that I was looking forward with keenest anticipation to the following Sunday, when I was to preach in his pulpit, and Mrs. Dahlberg and I were going with the Vernons to their lakeside cabin after the service. During the week we contacted each other to arrange about the hymns, the Scripture lesson, and other details of the worship service, agreeing that we would meet together a half hour early on Sunday morning for any last minute consultation.

At the appointed hour I drove up to the Church of the Open Air, only to be met by a delegation of sober-faced laymen.

"We have been waiting for you," they said. "Dr. Vernon died at midnight last night of a heart attack."

I was stunned. So likewise was the congregation. Only a few of his own church members had heard the news. When the announcement was made at the beginning of the service that their pastor had died during the night, a wave of sorrow like a great sigh out of the pine trees went through the cars in which the people were seated. But we went on with the service, and the following Tuesday I conducted Dr. Vernon's funeral in the First Congregational Church of Brainerd.

Naturally this experience underscored for us all his last impassioned message on the importance of living before we die. Dr. Vernon was right. Much of our preaching and singing is too other-worldly. While millions of people are dying in war and slavery on earth, waiting for someone to come to their rescue, we are content with the comfort of harps and pearly gates in heaven.

Jesus wanted us to have an abundant life in the here

LIVING BEFORE WE DIE

and now. The question which should occupy us most is not where we *will be* spending eternity but where we *are* spending it. Many people go through seventy or eighty years of life on earth without having lived at all. They act as if God did not exist. They never commit themselves to any great cause. They never take a stand on any moral issue. The fate of races and nations may hang in the balance in Montgomery, Alabama, or in the cities of Jerusalem and Cairo, but they are silent, inactive, neutral. They never come face to face with the Cross of Jesus Christ, nor plunge into any heroic effort for the kingdom of God. They are merely existing—dead while they yet live. They remind me of the old Pennsylvania Dutchman who when asked how long ago his neighbor died, said judiciously, "If he had shust lived until next Tuesday he would be dead two weeks already."

Of course it makes a great deal of difference what we mean by life. For some it means ambition and power. For others it means dissipation and indulgence—going out and having themselves a time. Jesus, however, in his last prayer with his disciples, made very explicit what life in the Christian sense really means. He said, "This is life eternal, that they might know thee, the only true God, and Jesus Christ, whom thou hast sent." The Apostle Paul, defining his concept of life, declared, "To me to live is Christ, and to die is gain." Putting it another way the writer of First John made it clear enough for any of us to understand. "We know that we have passed from death unto life, because we love the brethren. He that loveth not his brother abideth in death."

If we have gone through life without knowing God, therefore, or entering into a living, dynamic relationship with Christ and our fellowmen, we have not lived completely. Some of us feel that without Christ we could not have lived at all. The reason Christ rose from the dead was because he was so alive to God before he died.

To stress this fact of life *before* death is in no sense to minimize the truth of life *after* death. Death is a terrible reality. The Apostle Paul called death an enemy, and said that it was the last enemy that should be destroyed. We should not sentimentalize the fact of human experience. It robs us of those dearest to us, dims the light of the stars above us, and staggers us to the heart. What we believe about the future, therefore, and the glad reunion with those we have loved and lost awhile, makes a vast difference in the courage and joy of our living before we die. But, I repeat, we must live for Christ abundantly in the here and now, if we are to live in the hereafter.

How bravely some people can live before they die is illustrated by a man who addressed a pre-Lenten retreat of our St. Louis ministers two years ago. Our main speaker during the day was Dr. Harold Wilke of Cleveland, Ohio, who is head of the Evangelical and Reformed Church Commission on the Enlistment and Training of the Ministry. As he rose to speak I was impressed by a certain dignity, strength, and charm of personality that I could not explain. Then I became aware of the fact that he was a man without arms. Both sleeves were empty, and thrust into the side pockets of his coat. Then came an amazing revelation. From my seat at one side of the front of the chapel I was able to see him suddenly slip one foot out of his shoe, as he stood back of the pulpit. His foot was encased in a kind of fingered glove. Without a moment's warning, as he stood on his left foot, he lifted his right foot to the top of the pulpit desk and turned the page of his Bible as deftly as one of us would do it with the hand. There was no embarrassment about it. Hardly anyone seemed to notice it.

Then he told the story of his life. He had been born without arms. Eager to go into the ministry, he had been flatly discouraged by every minister he had talked to. "Why, it would be impossible for you to perform even the simplest physical duties as a pastor," said one. "How would you baptize anyone, for instance?" But he persisted. He went through college and seminary, and had a notably successful pastorate. Then he took a course at the Karl Menninger Psychiatric Clinic in Topeka, Kansas, after which he became a chaplain in a veterans' hospital, where he exercised an unusual ministry among crippled and disabled men. Today he is the head of the commission in his denomination which has the whole responsibility for recruiting and training men for the ministry—the very ministry from which he was nearly rejected.

How does he baptize a baby? Even though I am a Baptist, and a member of a denomination which does not practice infant baptism, I was never more deeply moved than when I heard Dr. Wilke describe his baptismal service. Having memorized the service, he does not need a book. All he asks of the parents or the godparents is that they hold the baby a bit higher than usual at the baptismal font. When the moment comes for the actual baptism, Dr. Wilke bends over, kisses the baptismal water in the font, and with the water still clinging to his lips, stoops down, kisses the baby on the forehead, and says, "I baptize thee, in the name of the Father, and of the Son, and of the Holy Ghost."

What could be more beautiful and holy? I can imagine that when Harold Wilke was born, and his father and mother found that he was born without arms, they might well have said in their bitterness and despair, "It would have been better that our son had died, or not been born at all." But out of their cross, and his cross, has come an incomparable resurrection. He can read, he can write, he can feed himself, shave himself, and open doors, without hands. He can open doors into the human heart that no one else can open. He is living the abundant life, *before* he dies. We may be sure that that kind of a life will go on forever, in the next world as well as here. Death will be but an interruption.

We have at our house an electric clock, with a particularly sweet and beautiful Westminster chime. One evening as I was at the telephone, just at six o'clock, I heard the clock striking the hour. At the moment when the chimes were on the upward swing of the melody, the power went off, plunging us into darkness and complete silence. The power was off in our whole area of the city, for nearly half an hour. Suddenly the lights went on again, and we could see. But what impressed me most was that the electric clock resumed its music precisely where it had left off, on the upward notes of the melody.

So shall it be in the resurrection. When death comes, if we have lived vitally and believingly in this life, that seeming death may shut off the power for a time, break into the music of life, and plunge us into darkness and bewilderment. But when the power goes on again, and the light of the risen Christ shines about us, I believe we shall hear once more the upward beat of the music, and look into the face of the Savior who stooped down to kiss us with the baptismal waters of God's love. Let us live more nobly, then, *before* we die, because we shall so surely live forever *after* we die.

4

THE LIVING CHRIST

by O. A. GEISEMAN
Pastor, Grace Lutheran Church, River Forest, Illinois

LUKE 24:1-12

CHRIST was nailed to the Cross at nine o'clock on Good Friday morning. He departed this life at three o'clock on the afternoon of the same day. Events followed with lightning rapidity. His friends took his body down from the Cross. They wrapped it in burial linens and laid it in a tomb. There was no time for the customary formal rites which were bestowed upon the dead as a mark of respect and love and honor. The Sabbath Day was only a few hours away. Anyone who touched a dead body on a Sabbath Day made himself ceremonially unclean and thus was not able to participate in the observance of this day.

The Sabbath Day was, for the disciples of our Lord, a very dark and gloomy day. They felt that they had lost their Lord, their master, and leader. At the dawn of Sunday, women who had been devout followers of Jesus gathered their spices and ointments and hurried off to the tomb to perform the last rites for which there had been no opportunity on the day of our Lord's death.

When they came to the tomb they discovered that the great stone which covered the opening of the tomb had been rolled away. This stone, shaped like a disk, had been placed before the opening of the tomb and sealed by the Roman soldiers. Now it was gone. When the women looked into the tomb they discovered that it was empty. They were informed by the angels of God that the Lord was no longer there. These angels said, "Why seek ye the living among the dead? He is not here. He is risen." When the women heard this news they hurriedly returned and reported it to the apostles.

It is because of the fact that Jesus arose that you and I are gathered here this morning to commemorate and to celebrate this great occasion. If we were in Russia today attending one of the few remaining great churches, all of which probably are packed to capacity and whose audiences are all standing through the service, we would hear the ministering priest say: "Christ is risen!" And we would hear the entire congregation respond with a shout: "He is risen, indeed!"

Probably there is someone in this audience who is inclined to say: "I don't believe that. If Jesus really died, then I don't believe that he actually arose." Well, if there is such an one in our audience, then this is not anything unusual or new. Even the disciples of our Lord didn't believe it when the women came and told them that Jesus had risen. "Their words seemed to them as idle tales, and they believed them not."

But this doubt and unbelief did not prevail for long, for the apostles themselves went to the tomb to see whether or not the report really was true. They looked in and with their own eyes discovered that the tomb was empty. Not long thereafter they had the opportunity of walking and talking with the Savior. They dined with him. They heard his further instructions in the days which he spent on earth before ascending on high. They stood by and watched with awe and amazement as he did ascend to sit at the right hand of the Father. When the Spirit of God was poured out upon them at Pentecost there was no

THE LIVING CHRIST

truth of which they were more sure than the fact that Jesus did live, that he did arise, and that theirs was truly a "living Christ."

It was for the very purpose of sharing this message with people in the world of that day that everyone of these apostles went forth to proclaim the resurrection of his Lord. There came a day when they had to make a choice whether they would stand by this truth and die, or whether they would deny that truth and save their lives. Each one of these apostles, one after the other, laid down his life in confirmation of the fact that Jesus was a living Lord.

Now the fact that Jesus is a living Lord is a very important fact, and if you do not believe it then you will do well to do as the apostles did—have a good look. Let the Spirit of God tell you what happened. See how the living Christ has expressed his abiding presence in the life, the work, and the history of his church and in the many works of charity and adventures of love, which have grown out of that church. This is one of the astounding chapters in history—how Jesus, as the living Christ, has continued to make his love come to the lives of men. He is not dead. He lives!

The fact that he lives carries with it infinite meaning for each one of us. First of all, it means that he fulfilled the prophecies which had been made concerning him. The prophets of old had said that the body of the Messiah would not disintegrate. When our soul "shuffles off this mortal coil," it is not long before the body disintegrates. With us it is true: "Dust to dust and ashes to ashes." But with Jesus our Lord this was not true.

This is what the prophets had foretold. Jesus himself had said in speaking to his enemies and talking about his own body, "Destroy this temple and in three days I will raise it up again." This was a very defiant statement. He had told his disciples that after his death he would arise and that he would be with them, conversing with them, and revealing himself to them as the living, the risen Lord. All of these prophecies found their fulfillment, and thus as Paul said, "Jesus was declared to be the Son of God with power by his resurrection from the dead."

This great fact that our Lord arose also has immediate present meaning for each of us. Not only does it prove that he was what he claimed to be, but it also shows that he achieved what he came to do. Jesus came into this world to save us from our sins. I don't know what this means to you. If you are the kind of a person who looks into the mirror and admiringly winks at himself and says, "Ah, you are really good. There's nothing wrong with you. You make no mistakes. You commit no wrongs," then, of course, you are not interested in the fact that Jesus came to save men from their sins. But if you are honest, if you are more realistic, then you will know what men have always known throughout history: that they are not good, that they are all guilty, that they have all come short of the glory wherewith they could stand in the presence of their Maker and find his approval.

That is why we often experience a sense of guilt and out of the sense of guilt there flows a sense of fear. It is as Shakespeare said, "Our conscience doth make cowards of us all."

There are people who try to cope with the problems of sin in their own way. They don't want to call it sin. They try to give it another name which doesn't sound quite so bad. There are people who think that they can overcome the problem of fear and the sense of guilt by lying on a psychiatrist's couch. No matter how much you verbalize your sense of guilt and the reasons for it, and no matter

THE LIVING CHRIST

how long you make your story as you tell it to the psychiatrist, this will never prove the answer to your sin. Sin is a very real problem and something very real has to be done in order to solve this problem. That was why Jesus came. That was why he died for us on the Cross. The wages of sin is death, and only Jesus could pay this price for every member of the human family. This he did and by his resurrection he delivered the evidence that he, and not sin, had triumphed.

This is a message designed to bring comfort to the heart of every one of us. I have no way of knowing what kind of a life you may have lived. Some of us may have lived a very shabby kind of life. Some of us may have lived as though we were not humans, but animals. We may have lived without God, without prayer, without the sacraments, without any concern for our immortal souls, behaving ourselves as if we had only a body as an animal has. This is possible, and many people are living like that. Maybe we have even thought that it was sophisticated to be a bit promiscuous in matters of sex and to overindulge in the use of liquor. Probably we have thought that we were very smart and clever if we made some fast deal which wasn't altogether honest and on the square.

It matters not whereof you have made yourself guilty. When Jesus died on the Cross and rose again the price was paid. This is what the Bible means when it says, "God so loved the world that he gave his only begotten Son, that whosoever believeth in him should not perish, but have everlasting life." This is what the Bible wants to assure us of when it states that "the blood of Jesus Christ, God's Son, cleanseth us from all sin." This is what the Holy Scriptures are saying when we are told, "He was delivered for our offences, and raised again for our justification." Because Jesus is a living Lord, you and I have an assurance that our sins have been taken care of and that each of us in Christ can be absolutely sure of God's mercy, God's love, God's forgiveness.

The fact that our Lord arose not only reveals that he fulfilled Messianic prophecies concerning himself and that he worked out the redemption of our souls from sin, but it also makes us sure that we can and should be triumphant over death. Man through the ages has always been aware of the fact that one day he must die. The beautiful orchids some ladies are wearing this morning are not worrying about the fact that in a few hours they are going to be wilted and dead. Any pet parakeet you have at home is not spending the day in gloom worrying about the fact that in a few short years he will not be living any more. Death does not worry plants and animals, but it has always been a great problem for man, because man has known that he must die.

It is possible for us probably to postpone death because modern medicine is doing a great deal to prolong life by a few years. You ladies can create an illusion of having preserved your youth. You can have your hair dyed. You can have wrinkles removed by plastic surgery. You can deftly apply paint and varnish and thus preserve an illusion of youth. We men can take steam baths and sun baths and massages and exercise to keep ourselves young and a bit more vigorous. Now this is all possible. But no matter how much you can do in this respect, finally there comes a day when the grim reaper raps at your door.

This has always been a problem for man. Man has lived in fear of this, and it was for the purpose of liberating man from this enslavement that Jesus came. He came to break the bonds of death, to throw wide the gate of the tomb, and to make it possible for you and for me to arise unto eternal life. When you and I know that Jesus lives and that he's our Savior, that he died for us and rose for us, that his victory is our victory, then we have an assurance which enables us to live life with complete confidence. Then we need not spend our time in morbid worry about death. We need not go through life as though the sword of Damocles were constantly hanging over our heads. Then we can live with courage, with assurance, because we know death no longer has power over us.

It is this truth which makes it so wonderful to be a Christian pastor. We often have occasion to go into the bedrooms of people who are in great trouble. When we call on someone who is suffering from muscular dystrophy or multiple sclerosis or someone whose body is all twisted and distorted, or when we call on someone who by reason of war or an accident has been crippled and mutilated, we are calling on folks who know that they are not going to get up again. They are not going to be able to move around freely and use their limbs and muscles as people normally can. What a wonderful privilege to be able to go to people like that and say to them, "Chin up! Have a smile on your face. There are better days ahead. There will come a day when you will arise and when your body will be like unto the glorified body of the risen Christ."

The fact that Jesus has defeated death and brought to us the gift of life has meaning not only as it applies to eternal life, but also as it applies to this life. When the love of the living Christ moves into your heart, it begins to displace the things that are in your heart. As the love of the living Christ comes in, selfishness, inconsiderateness, cruelty, pride, arrogance, dishonesty, irreverence—all of these things must move out because the love of Christ is taking over. And when the love of Christ takes possession of your heart, then you become a new person and you have the capacity to live a new kind of a life.

O. A. GEISEMAN

This happened to a man like Zacchaeus. He was a thieving kind of individual, but when Christ came into his life and the love of Jesus took over his heart, he became a new man, an honest man, a new citizen, who restored what he had stolen, and who shared with the needy.

Mary Magdalene probably was a woman of the street, but when she encountered Christ and his love came into her heart, she became a very beautiful and dedicated daughter of her Savior. There are many women like that in the world today, women who one time lived a life of shame but into whose hearts came the love of the living Christ and who today are loved and honored wives and mothers living the kind of life a daughter of Christ ought to be living.

Paul at one time was a proud, cruel, arrogant person, but when he encountered the living Christ and Jesus got his love into Paul's heart there came to Paul a tenderness which was like that which we usually associate with a mother's love. Here was a man rugged and tough, who could take the blows of life, and surmount difficulties before which many others would have wilted, and yet he could write I Corinthians 13, a beautiful psalm of love. He was now a man of tender soul, because Christ had come into his heart.

This is happening to others and this is what God would like to have happen to you and to me. You and I do not need to accept ourselves where we are today. We do not need to remain the same kind of unlovable, unlikable people we now might be. As the love of Jesus comes into our hearts, we can begin to live a new kind of life. The living Christ can help you become the kind of a person God meant you to be. Such is the purpose of Easter. Such should be your experience this day!

5

OUT OF THIS WORLD

by J. WALLACE HAMILTON

Pastor, Pasadena Community Church,
St. Petersburg, Florida

"In my Father's house are many mansions: if it were not so, I would have told you."

—JOHN 14:2

FRANCIS BACON had on his bookplate an engraved picture. It was the picture of a small ship sailing out between the great Pillars of Hercules into an uncharted, unknown sea. Inscribed on the bow of the ship was its proud and defiant name: *More Beyond*. Well, that has always been the exhilarating faith of Christianity about all life in general. And on Easter Day it gets sharply focused on the particular matter of the soul's immortality: "More Beyond."

Easter is the triumphant affirmation of something we have never proved but instinctively feel, that here on this tiny, whirling planet, a satellite of the sun, we are creatures mysteriously allied to eternity; that this little world of time and space is a small fragment of something much larger than itself, an eternal life that includes this life; that we cannot live in this world aright until we see it as a kind of outer corridor of the Father's larger house.

"In my Father's house," said Jesus, "there are many places. If it were not so, I would have told you."

I do not believe that this Easter faith is diminishing in

mankind. The idea that belief in the future life is a primitive superstition, fast losing ground as civilization advances and knowledge increases, is an exact reversal of the facts. True, there are many crude ideas about immortality, and the idea itself has gone through many changes and some diminishment in spots—with the emphasis on man's animal ancestry, with social revolutions that scorn the heaven of the future and set out to make a heaven here, and so on. Nevertheless, not many people—ignorant or learned, are willing to stand at the grave of a loved one without at least a vaguely held hope that this age-old faith is true. Because God, as Pascal once said, has planted this belief in the instinct, and however much we try to disbelieve it, it keeps emerging in our thoughts when we come face to face with the mystery of death.

Now I have never been much impressed with the so-called proofs of the resurrection, or arguments for immortality, because I believe the Easter message means much more than that. The Christian view of immortality is not the mere assurance that life continues, as Dr. William Adams Brown once said, "but the revelation of the kind of life worthy to be continued." Every Easter I talk about that. But I am taking this path this morning as a kind of a concession to something that is very much in the atmosphere, the awakened interest in worlds beyond this.

This is the first Easter in human history in which man has succeeded in getting out of this world on his own steam. Our newspapers and magazines are full of talk about that, some of it wise, some of it very otherwise. But it *has* revived a sense of wonder, deepened the sense of magnitude, and vastly widened our thoughts about infinity —more beyond, other worlds beyond this one. I want to speak of the Christian hope of immortality against the background of a widened thought about infinity.

OUT OF THIS WORLD

Let's begin at the bottom rung of the ladder. Wherever you turn in this visible world you find strong hints of the invisible, the infinite. There is no limit to anything. Just start with that. Every excursion man makes into any realm of knowledge leads him very quickly beyond his depth into a wide ocean of infinity where the Pillars of Hercules stand pointing to the more which lies beyond.

Take the simple matter of counting—one, two, three, four. There is no end to that. A little boy proudly announced to his mother that he could count to a hundred. There is more beyond that. Keep counting. No matter how far you count, there is always a number larger than the last one you thought about. No limit—either way. There is as much below zero as there is above it. You can go down as far as you can go up. In every direction is infinity. You remember what Einstein said in his autobiography about why he turned from mathematics to physics. "I saw," he said, "that mathematics was split up into numerous specialties, any one of which could easily absorb a whole lifetime." Take up any study—rocks, trees, sea shells, music, and you'll soon find yourself out of this world, fingering the fringes of the infinite. The atom is an endless ocean. An astronomer, with his glass turned toward the sky, said, "We have discovered there are no fences, no limits, no boundaries." Follow the trail of anything and it leads you to the infinite.

Some people are sensitive because they are hard of hearing, or because they can't see as well as they used to. They should not be sensitive about that. We're all deaf and dumb and blind, some of us more so than others, that's all. We all live with limited senses in a limitless universe. Our human senses are even weaker than in some animals. If a man could see like an eagle, he would need no glasses for his eyes. If a man could smell like a hound dog, he could get the fragrance of a rose bush a mile away, and some other odors too. If a man could hear like a deer, we would need no amplifying system in this sanctuary.

Have you ever thought how awful it would be if our senses were not limited? It is a merciful arrangement of providence that we can't hear or see too much, that this delicate nervous system is guarded and insulated against more sensation than it can bear. If all the reality around us could break through the guard it would burn us out, as too much electricity blows a fuse. Yet in spite of that, here is man chafing under the limitation of his senses, trying to extend them by all sorts of devices, because he can't be content to live in a world where there is so much and get so little. You see, infinity is in the man too.

Now this is such a fascinating thought, let's explore it a bit. The ear, for example, is a wonderful receiving set. That's what it is—a little radio, a receiving instrument more intricately designed than any radio. The ear opens out on a world that comes to us as sound with a range slightly longer than a piano, between sixteen vibrations and eighteen thousand. That is, what we can hear with our ears is about eleven octaves. But we know there is more beyond that. That is only a small fraction of the sound there is around us. Most sound is either too high or too low for the human ear to catch. Little insects emit sounds that we can't hear at all. We thought we were very smart when we discovered radar, sending out sounds of high frequency, having them bounce back, until we learned that bats have been doing that for centuries. The bats have always known about radar and have used it for night flying. We *are* glad we have ears, but we're all very deaf. All we can hear with this small, built-in instrument is about eleven octaves of sound.

Move up the scale to where waves vibrate with higher

OUT OF THIS WORLD

frequency and we have another little receiving set—the eye. It is the television of the body. It opens up to us the world that comes as light and color. With this instrument, we get one octave more, just one octave, as Newton proved when he passed light through a prism, as we see when we look at a rainbow. Below the red of the spectrum we can't see; above the violet of the rainbow, we can't see. We can see one octave, one small peephole in a vast range of light.

Between these two worlds, between the world that comes to us as sound and the world that comes to us as light, there is a range of many octaves, sounds we don't hear, colors we don't see. Here are the heat waves, the infra-red—below the red. Here is the region where radio and television operate, long wave and short wave—a whole wave world that we can get in only with the aid of electronic instruments, except the little we get through the sense of touch.

When we go up above the level of seeing, we're in a limitless expanse of reality beginning with ultra-violet rays, going up through X-rays—called so by Roentgen, their discoverer, because he didn't understand their nature; then up through gamma rays emitted by radium; then up through cosmic rays which nobody yet knows much about; and so on, up and up into infinity. Our visible spectrum is approximately one forty-fourth of the wave lengths between cosmic rays and long electrical oscillations, which, as one physicist suggests, is "like trying to play a piano with two keys."

I like to think of this incredible creation of God as an organ, a vast, cosmic pipe organ which no master yet has mastered. Man has played on a few stops, made a few starts here and there toward infinity. He has experimented with about seventy octaves in the scale. But with these human instruments, this unaided body with its present sense equipment, we can bring in slightly more than twelve octaves, one of light and eleven of sound, approximately. To most of the world's reality we are wholly oblivious. We are all deaf and dumb and blind.

If we could really see we would not recognize the world we live in. If we could really hear, these flowers would be singing for us this morning, for color is sound we can't hear. Someone has invented a gadget to transform orchestra music into kaleidoscopic colors. You see the music as you hear it. The rainbow would come to us as a symphony of sound as well as a symphony of beauty. And the sun rising on this Easter morning would fill the earth with the "music of the spheres." The Old Testament poet said, "The morning stars sang together." That is literally and physically true. All motion is sound.

Small wonder man chafes under the limitation of his senses. Small wonder the hope is born in him that some day he will see more, that some day we shall really hear. As Plato said, we are like people living in a dark and shadowed cave. Through the narrow gateway of the senses we get out of the cave a little. Through two small peep holes of eye and ear we get a hint of the infinity around us. Shall we never get out of the dark, never get beyond twelve octaves, never know anything about our Father's house except what we can get through two little narrow slits?

"Now we see through a glass dimly." Then . . . "I tell you," said Paul, "eye hath not seen nor ear heard, neither have entered the imagination of man the things God hath prepared," already prepared, already real—infinity all around us.

Now when we move up out of the realm of the purely physical, if we can properly call it that, into the still more

OUT OF THIS WORLD

elusive realm of mind, thought, spirit, the strong hints of the infinite are themselves almost infinite. Back in the quiet study of the laboratory, the brain men of this century have been doing an amazing thing which has introduced a whole new era. They've been gradually rubbing out the line between matter and energy, between the visible and invisible, until where the physical ends and the spiritual begins is almost indistinguishable. And as they push their inquiry back—out and out to the far, dim edge of things—they find themselves walking the borderland of an almost unknown, uncharted, invisible world, which they can describe only in abstract symbols.

Thought! "What is thought," asked Eddington, "that strange being that dwells in the depths of everything?" Thought! No one has ever seen it, but it has transformed the fact of the earth. How fast can thought travel? Certainly the quickest way out of this world is by the power of thought. It needs no wheels or wings to arrive anywhere. I can stand here and in much less time that it takes to tell it, I can travel in thought to Canada, to Europe, to Africa. I can see the mission where my sister lives. My mind will move there instantly. If I take my body along as baggage, that is more complicated and expensive. In thought we can reach the moon, or Mars, in the twinkling of an eye. We haven't yet devised the machinery to get our bodies there. Shall we some day have bodies to match the mind? Will the spiritual body Paul talks about in I Corinthians be a body free from the limitations that mark it now, the pull of gravity, the effect of heat and cold, the process of aging and decay? Shall we have bodies that will move in instant obedience to the mind? And would that be any greater miracle than what we have now—bodies equipped for this world, and prisoned to it?

Now it is up in this invisible world of thought and mind

and spirit that the word "infinity" begins to take on moral meaning. And we begin to coin words which give immortality a character, a timeless quality, not merely in the sense of continuance but in the deeper sense of moral permanence. Here we get the hint of things eternal— eternal in the sense that they are lasting, indestructible. "The things that are seen," said Paul, "are passing, temporal. The things that are not seen are eternal."

We could get out of our depth here, but let's stay where we can handle it. Memory is a little hint of it, that marvelous power that preserves impressions through various changes of the body. The body passes—it is temporal. Memory lasts. I don't have the same body that I had when I was a baby, or a child, or even when I came first to this church twenty-nine years ago. Not a single particle remains—all gone. But I can remember well things that happened twenty-nine years and several bodies ago. Something there is, even in this life, that outlives and outlasts the body. Influence is another hint of it, that unseen force that goes on exerting power after the body is gone. In the books we have on our shelves, for example; every day we hold fellowship with the minds of other people, many of whom have long since passed from the earth but who still live and speak in their lasting influence.

Love is an eternal quality—invisible, immortal, and by its nature moves in an area where death cannot destroy or diminish it. Truth is eternal. Truth can't be destroyed.

> "The ages come and go,
>   Destruction lays our mighty cities low,
>   But truth caught up and flung against the sky,
>   Truth does not die."

This morning I read two things before I came to church —the front page of the newspaper, and the story of the first Easter morning. These women coming down early in the morning wondering about that stone—who will roll away the stone? Truth had received a mortal blow on Friday, and was sealed there in a tomb. How often that story is repeated. And then they discovered that God doesn't pay much attention to our little stones, who rolls them or who seals them. And Easter comes around once a year to vividly remind us how silly it is to suppose that God's truth—God's eternal truth, can ever be beaten down or buried in a tomb. "My Father's house," He said.

> This is my Father world,
> O let me ne'er forget,
> That though the wrong
> Seems oft' so strong,
> He is the Ruler yet.

And this is what puts character into immortality, this moral quality, the character of God, the trustworthiness of God. It's the Father's house we live in. Infinity by itself is terrifying. The infinity that science is opening up today is frightening. That is why, as Dr. Hocking in his new book, *The Coming World Civilization,* says it is imperative now that we get our science and our religion together. Science without religion means suicide. Pure science leaves us with a soulless universe, a universe without heart, without love, without moral meaning, without character.

Suppose we did get to other planets. What could we do there? Men are talking rather glibly now about conquering outer space. Getting out of this world has become a new game for man to play. And it *is* quite an achievement—getting out of this world, putting moons in the sky, even little ones. And we have a vague feeling that we have stepped into a new era with many surprises ahead. But

J. WALLACE HAMILTON

man is not going to conquer outer space or get out of this world very far; not with these bodies we won't. We are not going to be flying about in interstellar space, "going from galaxy to galaxy" as I heard in a speech a few weeks ago. We may get to the moon or Mars, maybe soon, learn something about the near planets. But visiting the planets of other suns to hobnob with the natives there, that is something else. Those immensities are simply paralyzing to the human mind, and greatly underestimated by some enthusiasts. To get to the nearest star, traveling with the speed of light, would take four and a half years. And to get to other galaxies means the crossing of great gulfs which light itself takes millions of years to cross.

Man does not live that long. That is not going to happen, in a few years or in a few hundred. We are simply not made for the immensities, nor equipped for infinite distances. Man is a frail, earth-bound creature, frightened by the limitless, for he has neither the physical nor emotional equipment to cope with it. Think of being out in space with a human body halfway between here and Mars. Test pilots are now submitting to laboratory experiments simulating conditions of space travel, the problem of weightlessness, hunger, heat, cold, loneliness, mental depression in being completely isolated from the earth. Most of us couldn't stand that. Infinity by itself is simply terrifying.

Even this world gets too big for us at times with its terror and tensions, and especially when we forget that it is our Father's house we live in.

> Cradle the earth for a moment, Lord,
> In the palm of your healing hand,
> Whisper a soft, reassuring word
> That I can understand;
> For I am a lost and bewildered child,

> In a tangled, atomic maze,
> Troubled and easily beguiled
> By neon, noisy waves;
> Cradle the earth for a moment, Lord.
> In the palm of your healing hand,
> Whisper a clear and guiding word
> That I can understand.
>
> —Alice M. Swaim

And that's it! It was Christ who whispered the clear and reassuring word. "Don't be afraid," he said to a few men frightened with the possibility of losing him.

"Let not your heart be troubled, neither let it be afraid. You believe in God. You believe in me. You trust me. In my Father's house are many places: if it were not so, I would have told you. I go to prepare a place for you. And if I go, I will come again and receive you unto myself, that where I am, there you may be also."

And that word makes the difference. We don't know anything about heaven. We know no more about heaven than we know about the planets around the suns of Orion. For all we know, they may be one and the same thing. We don't know where heaven is or what it is.

But is it not enough to know it is the Father's house, a place prepared for a people—prepared? Some one has likened the experience of death which is a frightening thing to some, to the process of birth. To the unborn child, the prospect of coming into this world would seem a frightening thing. He would have great difficulty making clear to himself what this world is like. It would be so utterly different. He lives without air. How can he live with it? He lives without light. How can he live with it? If the unborn child were possessed of imagination, the prospect of birth would seem to him like death, being wrenched away from the familiar conditions which have sustained him.

Well God knew all that, so he prepared a place for him. When the new born child was first aware of anything, strong arms were around him, eyes were looking into his with love and tenderness. Some one had anticipated his coming. Hopes were centered on the happy day of his arrival, and he felt safe because some one had prepared a place for him. More than that, he was prepared for the place. All unknown to him he had been developing eyes for light he had never seen, ears for sound he had never heard, lungs for air he had never breathed. All unknown to him he had been getting ready for this place and came here prepared and equipped for a new order of life. "If God so carefully guards our entry into this world, will he be so careless about our entry into the next?"

"So," said Jesus, "don't be afraid. I will come and receive you, that where I am, there you may be also."

We come into this world all helpless and bare,
We go through this world in struggle and care,
We go out of this world, God only knows where,
But if he lives in us here, we shall live with him there.

Such is our faith. "More beyond." "Other worlds." "In my Father's house . . . many places." We don't know *what* is there, but we know *who* is there, and we put our trust in him.

THE EASTER MESSAGE

by MARTIN J. HEINECKEN

Professor of Systematic Theology, Lutheran Theological Seminary, Philadelphia, Pennsylvania

I CORINTHIANS 15:12-14, 17-20, 55-58

IT IS good that we are gathered here this morning in our Easter finery, gay and gallant, surrounded by the lilies which even Solomon in all his glory could not match, singing glad hallelujahs, looking up with shining eyes and saying, "Christ is risen! He is risen indeed!" For this is the day of triumph, of victory, of joy and hope, without which light itself would be darkness and fear and sorrow and loneliness our lot. If ever the preacher of the Gospel is put to the test it is today. "How beautiful upon the mountains are the feet of him that bringeth good tidings, that publisheth peace!" God forbid that there should be one false note in our symphony of praise, one quaver of uncertainty, one lick-spittle whine of apology, one hint of argument to bolster our unwillingness to surrender to the living God. If ever it must be clear that the Gospel is not just another of man's attempts to solve the riddle of his existence, but God's own answer to his predicament, it must be clear today. If ever there must be no mistake that the Gospel is nothing other than the good news of what God himself has done to put an end to man's misery, then it must be so today.

He who brings good news brings it to those who are in

distress and the measure of the distress is precisely the measure of the goodness of the news. If there is to be fullness of joy, the one must be as absolute as the other. We must be on our guard, therefore, lest we let the gay finery of this day blind us to the truth of who and what we are and of our true predicament in existence.

Even before this day is out the flowers will have faded, their sweet fragrance will have taken on the nauseous odor of corruption, the light of day will once more give way to the darkness of night, the songs of trumph will yield to all the noise and clangor of a world at strife, the aching will return to the heart, the voice of the accuser will again be heard, all the restlessness, the insecurity and the anxiety of our life, the fury and the fire, the bitterness and brutality, the lust and the longing, the smallness and the meanness, the regrets and the unfulfilled hopes—all the mixed-up confusion, from heights of lofty exaltation to unplumbed depths of despair, will return, and then it will be revealed whether we really know where to turn to hear once more, in the midst of the battle, the cry of victory, or whether we have only done what is the besetting sin of our day, covered over the ugly reality of life with a superficial veneer, dressed ourselves up and painted our faces to hide the hideousness of what we haven't the courage to own up to.

Let us then face our predicament honestly and consider the impossibility of the resurrection and God's prerogative to do the impossible, or, in other words, the absolute miracle of the resurrection as the answer to man's absolute helplessness.

We are all aware of the running battle through the centuries between organized religion and the advances of science, which continually increase man's power and seem to make reliance upon God more and more unnecessary.

THE EASTER MESSAGE

What a giant step from the days when puny man stood with only a club in his hand to defy all the forces of nature conspiring against him to today, when with the powers of his mind man has harnessed those forces to serve his will. From ox cart to jet plane, from flickering candlelight to the night turned bright as day, from hoe and rake and wind-swept threshing floor to tractor and combine and factories and food marts, from leeches and bloodletting to anesthesia, spotless hospitals, pretty nurses, heart massages, brain surgery and what not! Yes, and from the bow and arrow to the H-bomb and the absolutely devastating power at the beck and call of one man's whim. And now man is reaching into outer space and it is actually only a question of time until a trip to another planet will be as ordinary as catching the 8:15 to the office in the morning. Before this advance of science it seems as though the forces of organized religion have been beating a very disorderly retreat, trying desperately to salvage some little stronghold for God to which man would be forced in the end to find shelter from the storm.

But this sort of retreat is no good. Either we turn over the mastery to man and let him fix things up the sooner the better without any help from the skies, or else we recognize that the true human situation of man as the creature of God does not and cannot change with the years. Unless man, no matter how much he increases his power, recognizes his absolute dependence upon God at all times, and unless he lives in every moment in recognition of the fact that he is always under both the judgment and the mercy of the living God, he has not entered even into the forecourt of the holy of holies and he will have no cause for rejoicing on this festival day of the resurrection.

There is a good bit of confusion in these days about

the word "existential." To many it is a synonym for hopelessness and despair, the loss of all security in a mixed-up jumble of a world that makes no sense, like the pictures of the modern artist, which look more like the seat of the artist's pants after he has accidentally sat on his paint-smudged palette than anything done with a purpose. But this is a misunderstanding of what others mean by taking seriously man's situation in existence, when to exist means to stand out and be separated from and estranged from the true fount and source of our life in whom alone we live and have our being.

The existential situation, therefore, is nothing other than that situation in existence in which man as man, created in God's image, made in, for and by love, finds himself here in this bourne of time and space, when he is called upon to live his life from moment to moment in fateful decision either to do the will of his Creator and Judge or to spurn and defy that absolute Lord and when deep in his heart he realizes that he has already made the latter choice.

So man is in this life absolutely dependent upon the God who made him. There is nothing he has not received. He is suspended at all times over the abyss of nothingness from which he came and into which he would sink, not leaving the slightest trace, if he was not sustained at all times by the will of his Creator. Not until there has come to a man, be he pauper or prince, peasant or pope, this realization of his creaturehood, does he know what it means to exist before the living God.

What difference does it make, whether he be the first Adam looking with wide-eyed wonder at the world, at the sun that lights him by day and the stars and moon that are his guide by night, at the garden he is to till and the animals he is able to name and the woman that is his help-

THE EASTER MESSAGE

meet, or whether he be the Twentieth Century sophisticate peering through his telescopes at the distant galaxies or through his microscope at the myriad life unfolding before him! Before God he is nothing and less than nothing. Yet this God has given him a name and set his seal upon him and chosen him to be his son and to crown him with glory and honor and give him an everlasting habitation.

Nothing before God, yet the object of that God's most loving concern, so that if all others forsook him, yet the Lord would take him up! "Behold, he that keepeth Israel neither slumbereth nor sleepeth. The sun shall not smite thee by day, nor the moon by night. . . . The everlasting God, the Lord, the Creator of the ends of the earth fainteth not, neither is weary. They that wait upon the Lord shall renew their strength, they shall mount up with wings as eagles; they shall run and not be weary, they shall walk and not faint."

There are three points where man's absolute helplessness at all times must become apparent to him. The most obvious of these is death, the victory over which we are celebrating today. Death! What have we made of it? Once death was portrayed as the grim reaper, relentless with his scythe, sparing no man, haunting him in his most exalted hours and riding him like a demon even into the hours of his sleep.

Who that has ever loved the good earth, the salt sea air, the sun rising from the mountaintop after arduous climb, and all the myriad sights and sounds and touches of this life will consign himself without a murmur to death? Who that has ever loved a friend in whose company his soul rejoiced, so that, as St. Augustine says, "a flame was kindled which fused their very souls and of many made them one," will resign himself complacently to a parting that is forever? What man has ever loved a maid who did not feel that love such as theirs was never since the world began and that it would outlast all the ravages of time and fortune? Who has ever walked the city slums whose children have never seen grass or flowers, the dives where drunkards lie in their own excrement, the asylums where madmen rage and idiots sit with soulless stares, the waste lands where hunger and cold and heat put men to the rack, to say nothing of the ravages of war, who that has even a measure of awareness of the giant agony of the world, its unrequited sufferings and monstrous injustices, can resign himself with composure to the thought that there shall never be a reckoning and that only in death is there surcease from sorrow?

What man alive will not defy all this? Man is the animal who buries his dead and marks the graves and cannot forget that out of the earth new life always springs. The supreme sloth, someone has said, is not to want to live forever. "Do not go gentle into that good night," says Dylan Thomas, "Rage, rage against the dying of the light."

Death is man's last and bitter foe, but we have tried to dress him up and make a friend of him. We cover death with flowers and sentimental music and perfumed cosmetics. We hide away death. Try asking some of our younger generation how many of them have witnessed an actual death (and not its TV counterpart), the slow agony of it or its sudden horror and you will be in for a rough surprise, in spite of the pervasiveness of death. It is positively indecent to die in public. And then as if to mock our fastidiousness, death rains from the skies, 100,000 dead in one night of bombers over Dresden six days before the end of World War II.

How absolutely helpless we are before that last and bitter foe, the death rattle in the throat, the glazed eye, the

THE EASTER MESSAGE

lips that will speak no more, the cold and rigid limbs, the odor that in man is the most nauseating of all. Death is no different than when for the first time the first Adam stood before its mystery—Adam and Eve with their child in their arms, slain by a brother's hand! How could our human lot be portrayed more poignantly! Where has he gone and why, he who was such a delight, whose offerings rose as a sweet smelling savor unto the Lord? And why does that other one go on living, whose jealous wrath was the cause of this meaningless end? Yes, we can try in the face of death to be resigned, to square our shoulders and to take it. Time does heal the deepest wounds and out of suffering come strength and nobility. But deep within we know that there is something false about such bold defiance. Death we cannot handle. The moment we are born we are old enough to die and all our existence is existence unto death, running toward this end as surely as the rising sun is already turned toward its setting.

But there is another factor that makes death even more horrible. If death meant mere transition to another state of being, another phase of life, as the chambered nautilus leaves its outworn shell only to inhabit a statelier mansion, then why should it be feared or resented? Or, even if death means annihilation, why should man cringe before it, because, as the ancient philosopher said, "When I am, death is not, and when death is, I am not." But we cannot dismiss death so cavalierly for the Scriptures say, "It is given unto man once to die and after that the judgment." And also: "It is a fearful thing to fall into the hands of the living God."

Who are we then, simply to console ourselves with our wish-believings, when death means nothing other than to come face to face with our Maker and our Judge? If ever our absolute helplessness is clear to us, it should be clear to us now. How shall we stand before this Judge? In all the world's literature there are the stories of that final, fearful day of reckoning. It is not only that now the pitcher that has gone so long to the well is broken and all the life-giving water spilled out, but a creature of responsibility, entrusted with tremendous gifts, is called now to his accounting, the last and final reckoning, when it is forever too late to make amends.

Here the true nature of all sin is made clear to us and we see our absolute helplessness before it. If the history of the world's religions is anything it is the story of man's frantic and futile efforts to deal with his sins and somehow to make amends, to undo again what has been done, to call back the unkind word, to heal again the broken promise, to catch again the lost opportunity for good. "Wherewith shall I come before the Lord, and bow myself before the high God? Shall I come before him with burnt offerings, with calves a year old? Will the Lord be pleased with thousands of rams, or with ten thousands of rivers of oil? Shall I give my firstborn for my transgression, the fruit of my body for the sin of my soul?"

So there rises before our mind's eye the spectacle of man's religiosity from the Hindu who covers the whole length of India with his prostrations until finally he submerges his filth-encrusted bag of bones in the sewage-infested waters of the Ganges to the senseless scourgings of Luther in his monastery cell. And to what avail? To get forgiveness for having repaid a kindness with a hurt, for having pledged fidelity and then having broken troth, for having squandered a priceless gift or used for a needless, selfish indulgence what might have given another a moment of delight? How can you ever get forgiveness unless it is freely granted by the one offended and he who has been hurt by his own hurt makes it right?

THE EASTER MESSAGE

No! We might as well try to dip the ocean out with a spoon or pull ourselves up to the moon by our bootstraps, or point to the end of our finger with the end of the same finger, or make the darkness light, or turn death itself into life. No! Here we are at journey's end and at wit's end, here, before the judgment seat!

What a monstrous perversion it is, to seek to deny all this and to make of man nothing but a turmoil of chemicals in a pot with less responsibility than a beast driven by instinct or a stone hurled through the air. This is our boasted Twentieth Century progress that we who've brought so much under our control, have now ourselves been reduced to nothing but things thrown around by a thrower who himself is thrown by the things he throws. Then we have the effrontery to look with disdain upon the folly of bygone years when a man dared to stand before his God and confess: "Against thee, thee only have I sinned and done this evil in thy sight. Have mercy upon me, O God, according to thy lovingkindness: According unto the multitude of thy tender mercies, blot out my transgressions. Wash me thoroughly from mine iniquity and cleanse me from my sin." This is the second point of man's absolute helplessness, when he stands in the need of the forgiveness of sins.

The third point is that of his loneliness, which stands not unrelated to the other two. Because it is precisely when a man is with those he loves, with those with whom he has become knit by ties that only time and closeness can weave, friends, wife, husband, children—it is precisely in the moments of highest bliss that human companionship can hold, that man is overcome with "loneliness," which is to him the sign, that there is nothing that can satisfy his longing, short of the companionship of the living God.

This is the truth of Augustine's saying: "Thou hast made us, Lord, for thyself, and our heart is restless within us until it rests in thee." This is the cry of the psalmist: "My heart longeth, my soul fainteth for the living God. As the hart panteth for the waterbrooks, so my soul thirsteth for thee, O God. When I think upon thee in the night watches, my heart and my flesh crieth out. O that I might know thee and see thee face to face!"

How shall a man bring about that vision? How shall he unlock the fast-closed door? How indeed, unless God himself come to him and sit at table with him as an equal?

So this is the place of man's absolute helplessness and what answer is there, except the glad Easter cry, "The Lord is risen. He is risen indeed. O death, where is thy sting? O grave, where is thy victory? The sting of sin is death and the strength of sin is the law, but thanks be to God who giveth us the victory through our Lord Jesus Christ."

In our text there is a curious reversal of the usual order with respect to the resurrection of all men and the resurrection of Jesus. St. Paul does indeed begin his testimony with the simple proclamation of what had been delivered to him, how the man Jesus died, and how on the third day he rose again, and how this Risen One had appeared to his disciples. This is the news that could only be proclaimed of one who had passed into death and then had come again to show himself the victor.

There is no other way of accounting for the rise of Christianity. This is the united testimony of those who had lived and eaten with him during his earthly sojourn: "The Jesus whom you crucified God hath raised up." What could not happen and does not happen and what always raises shrill cries of derision from those who know a thing or two and will not be deceived by old wives'

THE EASTER MESSAGE

fables, this was here declared to be a fact: a sealed tomb sprung open, a lifeless body once more alive, not a spook or a ghost or a too-fond memory materialized into a shape, but this same Jesus with the nail prints in his hand, the spear thrust in his side and all the familiar marks of his earthly sojourn, the sound of his voice and the way he had of breaking the bread.

So this is the starting point and there is nothing to do but proclaim it in the only way that such news can possibly be proclaimed, as the most unbelievable of events without which there would be no gospel and men still without hope in the world.

But in spite of this, there is the curious reversal, which makes the general resurrection of the dead more basic even than the resurrection of the man Jesus. In simple words: Do all men rise from the dead because Jesus did? Or did Jesus rise from the dead because all men rise from the dead?

Let us try to follow Paul's reasoning. First he simply reports what has happened, but at the same time he interprets that event. This is not simply the occurrence of a most unusual phenomenon, as when today by some freak of circumstance a person believed dead comes back to life, or when by means of massage a heart that has stopped beating is put to its work again. What has happened is declared to be in accordance with the divine will in fulfillment of ancient prophecy. This is not just the phenomenon of a dead man come back to life any more than the death on the Cross was just the death of a brave man with the courage of his convictions, because such events would be repeatable and would have only limited consequences.

But what has happened here is of cosmic, universal significance. It is the crucial event of all history, which marks the turning point in the history of all mankind. It is like the crisis of a disease when at last its hold has been broken and the return to health begins. It is like the decisive battle in a war with all the skirmishes thereafter representing only mopping-up operations, no matter how fiercely fought.

St. Paul says simply, "He died for our sins according to the Scriptures," and, "He rose again according to the Scriptures." This means that here all the ancient prophecies and longings for a redeemer and indeed the hopes of all mankind have been fulfilled. Whatever false expectations there were of a "Messiah-king" who would set up an earthly paradise or of a Man from Heaven who would come in great power and glory to the consternation of the wicked and the joy of the just, here stand both corrected and fulfilled. This death on the Cross is the culmination of a life that was all suffering and all love and thereby atoned for the sins of the world: "Behold the Lamb of God that taketh away the sins of the world."

Therefore also that rising from the dead has an altogether different significance from that of a dead man come back to life. This rising again means the beginning of a new age of light and love and hope. "The people that sat in darkness have seen a great light and upon them that sat in the shadow of death hath the light shined." It means that death itself is conquered and has lost its sting. Whatever else death may mean, to him who has felt the holiness of God and taken seriously the absolute demands of the law, it can only mean the witness to his sin. It is not, as we have said, a transition to a higher stage, but it means the judgment, and only he who stands clothed in that strange and foreign righteousness of the one who loved him and gave himself for him can stand in that judgment, the fires of which will consume all unrighteousness.

So this resurrection is the only answer to man's utter

THE EASTER MESSAGE

hopelessness as he is faced by death and judgment. For here is the one who has conquered sin and death with complete trust in the heavenly Father, with absolute obedience and with a love that knows no bounds. Here, too, is the answer to man's loneliness, for it is his risen Lord who now is man's companion for the way. "Lo, I am with you always, even unto the ends of the earth." "Where two or three are gathered in my name, there I am in the midst of them." Not a distant God, but a God who shared with mankind all its pain and woe, and even now enters into the common elements of our daily life and is present to us: "The bread which we break, is it not the communion of the body of Christ. The cup which we drink, is it not the communion of the blood of Christ."

So we worship not a dead hero, but we celebrate the presence of a living Lord. This was St. Paul's first affirmation and then he went on to say, "If Christ is risen, then how say some among you that there is no resurrection of the dead." And then there follows that curious reversal of which we spoke, "If there is no resurrection then Christ is not risen," and if Christ is not risen, there follows all that chain of woeful consequences: Then ye are yet in your sins. Then they also which are fallen asleep in Christ are perished. Then Jesus is in fact nothing but a dead hero and if our hope in him is for this life only, then are we of all men most miserable.

This means then that to believe that a man Jesus once rose from the dead and came back to life without believing in the resurrection of the dead—*all* the dead—is like supposing that there could be a victory without an army to win that victory, that there can be light without a sun, a book without an author, a body without blood, a refreshing pool without a well-spring to feed it, a rose without a root, a building without a foundation, a son without a father.

MARTIN J. HEINECKEN

If there is no resurrection of the dead, that is to say, if there is no God who himself is the author of all life and light, and who alone can bring life out of death, then Christ is not risen either and then everything else is futile and vain. For man in the hopelessness of his predicament, there is no answer except the almighty power of God himself. Resurrection from the dead is no human possibility and neither is the forgiveness of sins, nor the satisfaction of his longings.

Only he who made the worlds and brought them into being out of nothing in the first place by the power of his creative Word is able also to say, "Little maid, I say unto thee arise! Lazarus, come forth! Hence death with all your terrors!" Remember that we are talking now, not of the immortality of the soul, which we can delude ourselves into thinking is our own inherent possession, a core that is incorruptible and not subject to mortality. No! St. Paul says, "This corruption must put on incorruption and this mortality must put on immortality."

This is a matter of the whole man come back to life. This is the most staggering and unbelievable of events. "The earth and the sea shall give up their dead." There is the valley of dry bones in Ezekiel's vision, "Son of man, can these bones live?" How shall they live, how shall they reassemble themselves and take on flesh and blood if there is not that God whose prerogative it is to do the impossible? Think of all that have ever lived and gone the way of all flesh, burned in the flames, disintegrated into nothingness in a flash by the power that man himself has developed, or gone back to dust and ashes through the processes of slow but sure decay! How shall they live again, if there is not that God who is the Lord of life, who shall wake them from sleep with his trumpet blast, clothe them with a body, even as he gives to each seed its

THE EASTER MESSAGE

fruit. And how shall they stand in the judgment, if there is not that divine advocate to plead for them, Jesus Christ?

So here is an end of it. This is the absolute miracle in which we rejoice today. It is God's prerogative to do the impossible, to raise us from the dead, to cover up our sins and the sins of all the world, and to open to us a future not burdened with that past, to create a new heaven and a new earth in which the tabernacle of God shall be with men and they shall have no need of the sun, for the Lord God himself shall be their sun, when faith shall turn to sight and we shall see face to face him "whom having not seen we have loved with joy unspeakable and full of glory."

This is the Easter message and we can only proclaim it. This is and remains the time of struggle, but the final victory is already won. There is an end of death and condemnation and there is a companion for the way. "Wherefore my beloved brethren, be steadfast, unmoveable, always abounding in the work of the Lord, knowing that your labor is not in vain in the Lord."

There is no proper ending to our Easter proclamation but this. To be sure, our ultimate hope is that eternal spring not followed by any winter, that eternal day after which there shall be no night. But there is still *today,* and in each *today* we must be resurrected from the dead, we must be born again to newness of life. Each day there is to be the death of sin and the birth of faith, the death of mistrust and hate and lust, and the birth of confidence and love and strength to do the good.

We are helpless also to bring this about, but it is God's prerogative to do the impossible, to send us forth from this house of God, not only clad in outward finery, but with a new heart for the old and with a will to meet in love the giant needs of the world.

7

THE CHRIST EVENT

by ELMER G. HOMRIGHAUSEN

Dean, Princeton Theological Seminary,
Princeton, New Jersey

"BUT now is Christ risen from the dead and become the first to rise of all who sleep the sleep of death!" This is the ringing affirmation of the New Testament. It is the militant declaration of the Christian church. Easter is true!

The whole Christian faith rests upon this joyous and daring testimony. Jesus Christ is alive, and all that he was and said and did and promised is validated by the mighty power of the Holy Spirit. He is Lord! The world was created by him; the meaning of life and history are in him; the consummation of all history will find the kingdoms of this world become the Kingdom of our God and of his Christ. The new age has not only broken into the world at his birth; it became present in his ministry; it is now the power of God raising men into the larger dimensions God always intended for them.

The first Christians faced their world with this startling message: The hour cometh and now is! The time is fulfilled! Accept the Easter fact and truth, welcome it into your lives, and rejoice in its eternal hope.

There is not one trace of misgiving about Easter on the pages of the New Testament. From beginning to end, it was written by men who did not guess at a possibility, speculate about a theory, or conjure up a vision. It was written by men who witnessed a reality which made a

THE CHRIST EVENT

world of difference for the world. It transformed the outlook of history. It was for them a day that changed the world. Something new was added which though surmised and hoped for, was not there before. The ordinary way of looking at things was shattered by a staggering event. This Christ was no longer the Jesus they knew, the sufferer whose light of life had been snuffed out on Calvary, and whose wonderful career had been liquidated by cruel powers. No, he was the center of things, the source of a whole new way of life. These early Christians were followers of a victorious Christian. They were enlisted in a triumphant army. They served a winning cause. They were on the offensive. They would not be intimidated by tyrannical powers whose violence could only kill the body. They knew this Christ to be the Lord of all power, whether natural, political, economic, or ecclesiastical.

The portrayals of Christ found in the catacombs, those underground sanctuaries and places of refuge from persecution, picture him always in his kingly power. He may be the Lamb slain by and for sinners, but he wears a crown on his head and holds a royal sceptre in the crook of his arm. He may be the crucified Jesus, but he reigns from the Cross. The followers of Christ who are called upon to suffer for his sake share the marks of Christ's victorious sacrifice. Like good soldiers, they rejoice in the wounds which are symbols of co-suffering with Christ in the battle for the cause.

Under no condition did those pioneer Christians think of Christ as a victim of evil circumstances; rather he courted the conflict; he took the battle to the enemy; he accepted the Cross as a part of his consecration for the sake of man's salvation. The evil passions of men did not bear down upon him and finish him off. Jesus laid down his life of his own accord! The prince of this world had nothing on him. He chose to drink the cup of suffering to the dregs. He was Master of every situation. He was a king, a victor, even in death. Easter is but the true sequel to his whole ministry; it is the full flowering of the Spirit's work in and through him. His confidence in the Father was vindicated. He was raised to the right hand of God's honor and power.

Little wonder that Paul could affirm: The eternal Yea has sounded in him. The divine approval of this Son is made manifest. And to those who are in Christ, life may be a grand pageant of triumph. They know through experience the same divine energy which raised Jesus from the dead. And though they walk as prisoners in chains through the imperial city of Rome, in their hearts they cherish the firm confidence that King Christ will triumph in every Rome in every nation on earth!

Easter is true as an historical event. It is a fact written indelibly into the annals of history. It happened! Historians may quarrel about the details of what happened on Easter as found in the New Testament records. What matter the details? The main thing is the *event*. We know that something of an unprecedented nature took place. It was as unique and crucial as the birth of Jesus in Bethlehem. Indeed, some would maintain that it was as unique an event as the creation of Adam. Did not Paul say that as in Adam all die, so in this Christ shall all be made alive?

The records are straightforward; they are the unstrained testimonies of honest men. Easter is not the result of mass hysteria; nor is it the product of wishful thinking. These disciples could not have stolen the body. Such a fraud is incredible in the face of the sterling sincerity of those martyrs. A fictitious invention of Easter is hardly to be considered in the face of the disciples' despair at his

THE CHRIST EVENT

death. A resuscitated, bleeding, emaciated Jesus would not have been able to free himself from his graveclothes, much less to evoke the high faith which those early Christians expressed in a victorious Christ. These disciples saw no ghost; they saw Christ alive! He was no illusion; he was real and actual.

But we are not only thinking of Easter as an historical fact. Easter is a grand event! A man returning from the dead is one thing; but Jesus alive is quite another! The resurrection does not stand by itself. It is not an addendum attached to the Gospel story. It is a part of the whole event of Jesus Christ, from his birth to his ascension. It is Jesus whom men saw! Any other man, even though he had died a cruel death, coming back to life might startle us with the miracle. Were some dead men to return, we might be frightened to a second death. The Christ event has meaning for us because of the person who was raised. You see, Jesus brought a new dimension to bear upon life. The disciples who associated with him heard strange things, they saw visions, they gained insights, as they followed him. Slowly, what was in Christ was communicated to them. They began to share in his love and righteousness and truth. The Christ event was restoring a lost dimension to their lives. To be sure, they had many things to learn. There was much that puzzled them. They were sensing the power of God whose primary intention is to move men from a "lost" life to a "saved" life. They were being taught some hard and difficult lessons in this school of life. But they were learning.

And then! The tragedy happened! The curtain came down on his life. And the generator of all that gave their lives such a wonderful sense of newness was murderously put out of the way on a Cross. This was their despair; they were faced with the ultimate tragedy. To whom could they go, now that the one who had the words of life was removed? The resurrection world, which Jesus had created in them, was about to be deflated. Little wonder Peter talked about going back to the old job of fishing. Little wonder the Emmaus friends hoped that Jesus would restore the glory of Israel. Their dirge could well be: Now is Christ dead, and he is the death of all who sleep the sleep of death! Yes, and the death of all who hope in life!

It is against this backdrop of despair that Easter must be seen. But now is Christ risen from the dead! This Christ dimension of life is not liquidated. This Jesus is alive! *The resurrection of Jesus Christ is the issue, not the survival of personality beyond death!* The whole event of his ministry is true; it is here to stay; it is not leveled down by the frightful status quo of secular powers. What Jesus had aroused in the disciples is not at an end. It has only begun! Though done to death by wicked and cruel men, he is not dead. The brightest and best hope of man has not gone down in glorious defeat at the hands of the ultimate tyrannies of the spirit of man. If Easter were not true, then the new life which he generates would have no validation. Better Jesus had never come to raise our sights to the heights, nor come to arouse our spirit to such high anticipations! The dark riddle of life would have been made worse by his coming into history and into life, if he had not been raised to complete what he had begun.

But his love is sovereign! He is not holden of the grave. He is victorious in the unending battle of man against the powers of darkness. He is let loose in the world where no hostile power can ultimately defeat him. The dimension he released into life is no illusion. He is no dated personality of the past. He is the Lord of history who lives still in the risen lives of his people. Easter is the very "core"

THE CHRIST EVENT

of the Christian faith. Yes, it is "the mightiest act of God in history," foreign to the common experience of men, inscrutable to scientific inquiry, and astonishing to believer and unbeliever alike. Dorothy Sayers, British playwright, author, and theologian puts it this way: "From the beginning until now, this is the only thing that has happened. When you understand this, you understand all prophecy and history."

Easter is a power. It is more than a fact and an event. It is dynamic with energy. This living Christ is the pattern, pioneer and power of the new life. He who is "in Christ," and in whom Christ lives, is a "new being;" old things are "finished and gone," as J. B. Phillips put it. The writers of the New Testament affirm with no hesitation whatever, that the self-same power that raised Christ from the dead may be shared and experienced by humans. Someone has said that the resurrection caused the world "to palpitate with new possibilities." The proof of Easter is in the Easter life. When Columbus was about to return after discovering a new land, he wondered how he could prove that he had seen strange places and people. To provide an irrefutable demonstration to skeptical Europeans, he took back with him several American Indians. These were proof enough! Words are of little value as compared with living reality. And Christianity has its proof of Easter. It is in the lives of men and women made new through the energy of Christ. Christianity is a religion of action and deed rather than of word. "The Word became flesh . . . and we beheld. . . ." The best proof of the risen Christ is the man in whom the dimension of resurrection life is an inescapable reality.

The powerful testimony of the early Christians was in its undoubted newness of life. Oh, they weren't supermen, by any means. Nor were they endowed with a kind of ethereal vitamin that made them more than their sinful and finite selves! But these real people knew the power of the same life that was in Christ Jesus. They knew they had entered into the realm of "eternal" life. Sad and discouraged, utterly deflated in hope, they had locked themselves in a secret room. They were imprisoned by fear and overwhelmed by the old enslaving tyranny of despair. And then, the miracle happened! Enter Christ! The lost dimension was restored; they began to move out into the world with a new sense of dignity, a new sense of destiny, and new sense of mission. It was Christ who made the difference. But he made the difference work in them. They became more than conquerors. From Christ's deathless love, they could not be separated. For them to live was Christ; to die was gain. The life and immortality which Christ had brought to light had brought light of life to them.

The Easter power has never been withdrawn. If anything, it has increased, and the signs of it are everywhere to be seen. Down through the centuries this Christ has been generating, raising and sustaining a generation of Easter people. He is the creator of the real Easter parade! The church is the long procession of Christ-raised people in and through whom the Easter event has become contemporaneous and relevant. Millions in our time know this resurrection power. It is valued most in areas where the age-old tyrannies of men laugh at the miracle of Easter, and in their pride attempt to liquidate the fact, the event, the power, the dimension of Easter. But still, it brings a song to the heart, a smile of hope to the lips, a thrill of joy to the soul. And no power on earth can arrest the progress of Easter. Lifted or raised up, Christ still draws men out of themselves into his glorious life.

He can take any man, stained by sin, cowed by con-

THE CHRIST EVENT

ditions, crushed by evil circumstances, and raise him to a new life. He may cause even the bitter memories of a life wasted and a body damaged to be woven into the fabric of that renovated life and make them into symbols of purity and messengers that make the grace of God more precious. Is such a process strange? Michelangelo could take a block of marble, lying on a dump heap, damaged by a fumbling amateur, and fashion even the chinks into a design of beauty. Is the great Artist of life to do less with precious human material? He has taken a fisherman and fashioned him into a pillar of the church; a tax collector and remade him into an apostle. And who can number the persons who have been lifted by the power of the living Christ! We can always name the great: Augustine, Luther, Ambrose, Francis of Assisi, Wesley, Witherspoon, and many another. But what of the countless unknown saints who have blest the earth by their Christ-raised lives and have injected into the life of the world the saving dimension of God's kingdom!

And what Christ can do for the individual, what he has done in history, he can do for his church in our time. Embarrassed and weakened by shameful divisions, entombed by sterile conventions, bound by meaningless habits of thought and life, enwrapped in the grave clothes of fear, and imprisoned behind walls of timidity and hesitancy, impotent to speak the living Word of the living Christ to an age that is eagerly waiting for the message of life—the living Christ can resurrect and revitalize such a church, put on her lips the ancient Gospel, fill her soul with a new communal life, and make her the source of hope in the world.

Easter is a hope. Thank God men are today concerned about hope. A miasma of hopelessness has subtly settled down upon the minds of many people. It is like a fallout of despair that threatens to fill the mind with deadly dread and terror. Many a person is inquiring about the future. Is there any rhyme or reason to history? Is life coming out anywhere? Is there any meaning to the jumble of events about which we read in our daily newspapers? Will the darkness close in on us? Is the universe heading for a grand finale in which all our aspirations and dreams will lie dead in the debris of a cosmic catastrophe?

This malady of despair must be met with the antidote of a Christian hope. Dr. Brunner has called hope the "oxygen" of the soul; without it we cannot survive. Military power and scientific discoveries and cosmic control are insufficient to give man this necessary ingredient for a survival with any meaningfulness.

Easter is true, declares the Gospel. This world is in the hands of a good God whose will for mankind is wholly benevolent. There is a power in history which does not let Christ and his people down. It is a daring thing for the Christian to point to Christ and say to the world: Here is the Lord. His is the last word. No power, whether temporal or spiritual, is able to defeat him. He has overcome the despair of the world. All things that are of any value are in him. He is their creator and the final pledge of their abidingness. All power is in his hands. No victory apart from Christ is permanent. Any victory apart from him is empty and futile.

No man can tell what the future holds. But the Christian believes that it will be with Christ. And whatever is happening today, or will happen in the future, is related to him and his purpose. The real issues of life and history revolve around him. Easter means that there is a power of love, of right, of truth, which is even now at work among men. It broke into the world in the person and ministry of Jesus Christ. He has gathered unto himself a com-

THE CHRIST EVENT

munity in which the Easter reality is at work. This is the church, the community of the resurrection. It is a portent as well as the advance guard of the social redemption of mankind. It is the saving remnant of society, the messianic community of history. It is a weak and frail, a finite and temporal, a sinful and human community, but it is one in which, according to Paul, all the fulness of God dwells. It is the steward and custodian of historical life, the body of Christ, the servant of God and the servant of man.

It must be evident that our present-day Christianity does not measure up to its mission and destiny. It hardly expresses the truth about Easter. It talks too much about the possibilities of eternal life when it ought to be demonstrating the reality of Easter. It is engaged in analyzing the situation, when it ought to be busy sharing its resurrection life with a world that is deflated of the substance of eternity. Instead of bolting itself behind closed doors, whether in dread of an enemy, or for fear of being contaminated by the world, or for lack of a militant faith, the church ought to be identifying itself with the world in the spirit of him who made himself a servant so as to enrich mankind by his ministry. It is high time we see Christ risen and, breaking through all the trimmings of a pagan Easter, which substitutes broken eggs for the sundered tomb and spring vitality for the rebirth of the soul, believe the Gospel and proclaim it with courageous abandon. For now is Christ risen from the dead and become the first to rise of all who sleep the sleep of death!

No words can improve on those which are so strongly put into poetry by Henry H. Barstow:

If Easter be not true.
Then faith must mount on broken wing;
Then hope no more immortal spring;
Then hope must lose her mighty urge;

ELMER G. HOMRIGHAUSEN

> Life prove a phantom, death a dirge—
>> If Easter be not true.
>
> If Easter be not true.
> 'Twere foolishness the cross to bear;
> He died in vain who suffered there
> What matter though we laugh or cry,
> Be good or evil, live or die,
>> If Easter be not true?
>
> If Easter be not true—
> But it is true, and Christ is risen!
> And mortal spirit from its prison
> Of sin and death with him may rise!
> Worthwhile the struggle, sure the prize,
>> Since Easter, aye, is true!

Easter is not only the hope for the future. It is the living hope for the present, a hope which is incorruptible and which does not fade away. In that hope we live and work from day to day.

8

SOMNOLENT SAINTS

by WILLIAM H. HUDNUT, JR.

Pastor, Third Presbyterian Church, Rochester, New York

CHRISTIANITY'S business is to wake men up; it is the religion of abundant, resurrected life. Yet as another Easter comes 'round, with its promise of reawakening for all of us, it is only fair to admit that many of us who call ourselves Christian have not been awakened. Instead, like the disciples in the garden, we have fallen asleep. A great torpor and spiritual inertia have come upon us, and we are languid, listless and supine. The world comes to us in the hour of its need, as Christ went to his disciples, and all too often finds us asleep.

Some Christians fall asleep from weariness in welldoing. They have been active in good works long enough and feel that they have done their share. Or they become weary because someone offended them or failed properly to recognize them when they were performing a good act, and so they lost interest. Or perchance they had to go to church too often when they were young, and grew so weary of religion that they have been spiritually asleep ever since. Such is the history of many a person who as a child could not feel what he was supposed to, and who as an adult has made no real effort either to feel it or to live it.

Without that saving generation of inner power, anyone will fall spiritually asleep. As G. K. Chesterton so wisely observed, it is not that Christianity has been tried and found wanting; it is that Christianity has been found difficult, and not tried. Spiritual slumber is much easier.

Other Christians fall asleep not so much from weariness in welldoing as from just plain weariness. The endless round of daily duties engulfs them; they dabble in many things and accomplish little. The test that they apply to their activities has to do not with their significance but with their congeniality, popularity and ease. They lead overbusy, scattered lives, and become involved in so many trivial affairs that they have no time or strength left to give themselves to any of life's great causes. When a person fails to do this, he has already fallen asleep spiritually, however full of activity his life may be.

Many Christians fall asleep spiritually because they are worn out by unresolved conflicts within their own lives. How easy it is for costly, inner yieldings to block us from God, to put our souls to sleep! The energy of many couples, for instance, is being dissipated because of needless marital strife. They could be reconciled to each other at the feet of Christ. But, instead, the husband is continually exhausted by undisciplined appetites and resentments, and the wife is constantly fatigued because of jealousy and temper. Nothing can put us to sleep spiritually much faster than the blighting effect of unsurrendered sins, unresolved tensions and unreconciled conflicts.

The glorious thing to realize, however, is that no soul is so asleep that it cannot awake to God. This is the Day of Resurrection, and it says to us that there is no life so dormant that it cannot blossom if only it will blossom for Christ. No spiritual lethargy need be permanent; it can be the empowering prelude to a stirring resurrection. This fact of fresh awakening is recognized by Matthew in the gospel narrative, and speaks to the very matter that we

SOMNOLENT SAINTS

have in mind this Easter morning. He writes that, after the crucifixion, "the saints that had fallen asleep arose."

There is a challenge here that should quicken and arouse us: no man need stay the way he is! The spirit of our risen Lord always shocks men into becoming new creations, and sleeping saints spring to life. Christianity's main business is to help men wake up to the great issues and see them from God's point of view. Suffering, for instance: how shall it be handled? The Gospel tells us that it need not defeat us, that it can empower us, that whenever love is crucified new life is born, and that with every crucifixion there can be a resurrection. Suffering is the inevitable prelude to and accompaniment of any great work of redemption.

However we may wish otherwise, America today cannot possibly help to save the world without suffering and sacrificing for it. When men suffer in a noble cause they come closest to the heart of God, for sacrificial love is the key to his nature. Write it down as a spiritual law: there can be no salvation apart from suffering, no happiness apart from sacrifice, no heroic and creative goodness apart from selflessness, no resurrection without crucifixion. Only as we die to ourselves can we live for others. Christ has power to make men live because he shows them how to die. No wonder the saints who had fallen asleep arose!

We need to awake to the great issues. The finest things in life never happen in sleep; they come when we are wide awake, on tiptoe. When we sleep we escape from reality. True Christianity is always an enhancement of reality until the sorrows, the cares and the problems of this world become our own. This does not happen in our dreams. "No man becomes a saint in his sleep," as Henry Drummond pointed out.

Someone has called the church the society of the holy

imagination, and I have heard definitions of it far worse than that. Imagining is not dreaming. It is a function of the mind, and when it is consecrated to furthering the fellowship of love it can do wonderful things. Shelley once wrote that "the great instrument of moral good is the imagination" and he was right. For without the ability imaginatively to put yourself in the place of another you will not feel for him, you will not care, you will not be led to help.

The creative spirits of mankind have always had great imagination. What they believed in was real to them, so real that they brought it to pass. They did not dream it up; they worked it out! Beethoven did not compose his symphonies in his sleep; he imagined them intensely, thought them through carefully, and heard them in his heart. True creation does not take place in our dreams.

Christians who are asleep to the great issues of life can never change this world as God wants it changed; this can be done only by Christians who are thoroughly awake. The gospel says that the saints who had fallen into the sleep of death rose up; they discovered life and hope and power, and so can we. That is what Easter means—a triumph over sleep and inertia and death; saints who have fallen asleep can rise to new life through the love of Christ.

Keeping spiritually awake is a continuing vigil. It is not enough to rouse the soul from slumber once a year or even once a week. It is a matter for daily attention. No soul can be a power for Christ unless it is constantly alert, ready to see spiritual opportunities in commonplace occurrences. Only the kind of love which is willing to be abased, to pocket pride, to serve people and never despair, can keep us from falling asleep. If we will open our lives to such love, and practice it, we will awaken spiritually

SOMNOLENT SAINTS

no matter how lethargic we may have been, and the awakened life in Christ that Easter celebrates will be a reality for us.

> "Ten thousand musics never could
> Stir an image out of wood;
> But let love knock at the church door
> And saints in niches, gray with lore,
> Step from their halos to the floor,
> And laugh, and are alive once more."

It is interesting to think of what might happen if we who call ourselves Christian were really to be awakened spiritually. Our homes, our church, our city might well become different places. How glorious it would be if every one of us who has fallen asleep spiritually were to rise with Christ to newness of life! Sometimes the first signs of resurrection are tenuous and tentative, as is illustrated in a paragraph from a friend's letter: "I should have notified Ripley that I have become a vestryman of a church. Believe it or not, 'tis true. You will also be surprised to learn that I have foresworn engulfing ardent spirits. This is almost a statement of fact!"

What this letter puts lightly is nevertheless a grand and serious matter, for it is a true picture of a somnolent saint waking up, of a dead Christian coming to life. Spiritual victory does not often come quickly or accidentally, but it does come whenever one who has fallen asleep rises up within himself, gives his life once and for all to God in Christ, and starts to do business with things that count.

What an influence a person can have when he is spiritually awake! I am reminded of a great old Christian crusader whom I used to know in the Adirondacks. He ran a family camp on Lake Pleasant and his name was "Pop" Tibbitts. Every morning, promptly at seven, reveille was sounded by a bugler. Then, a bit later, just to make sure, a bell was rung long and loud. The bell called the campers to chapel.

It so happened that one year who should take up a location near the camp but Gene Tunney, the heavyweight champion of the world. Mr. Tunney was, of course, a gentleman and a scholar, but not all of his ringside attendants and sparring partners could claim equal social and intellectual stature. The training quarters had not been there long before two worthy and pugnacious gentlemen from Mr. Tunney's entourage waited on "Pop" Tibbitts and told him that he would have to stop ringing that blankety-blank bell so early in the morning.

"Why?" innocently queried Pop.

"De boss don't like it," they replied; "he can't get no sleep. It's gettin' him all outa shape. He's gotta fight Dempsey, ya know, and he can't take no chances."

Pop knew the early-to-bed, early-to-rise habits of the abstemious Mr. Tunney and suspected that the chapel bell did not annoy him nearly as much as it did his sparring partners. So Pop told them that the bell would go on ringing each morning, as it had for many years.

A few days later a larger, more belligerent delegation waited on Pop and told him that he had to stop ringing that bell. Nobody could get any sleep at the training camp and they were not going to stand for it any longer. If he did not silence the confounded thing they would come over and wreck the place. Pop, challenged, drew himself up to his full height and said, "Boys, that bell has been ringing ever since I started this camp, and it's not going to stop now. It's a chapel bell. It rang long before you came, and it will ring long after you go."

Years later, on a transcontinental train, Pop and Tunney met again. They had not seen each other since that

SOMNOLENT SAINTS

memorable summer and Pop had aged. But he was still the jovial, indomitable Christian soldier, and he asked Tunney if he remembered him. Tunney looked puzzled for a moment, then a broad smile of recognition spread across his face. "Oh yes," he said, "of course I remember you; you're the man who rang the bell!"

How the world needs people who will ring the Christian bell, who without fear and with conviction will keep it sounding in their homes, their businesses, their communities, their world! The resurrection means little for us until we are individually summoned by it to a brave, new quality of life, until we personally answer the summons.

The saints who had been asleep rose up, "went into the city, and appeared unto many." That was proof of their sainthood—they went to work for Jesus Christ. When Montaigne was asked to be mayor of Bordeaux, he replied "I am willing to take the city's affairs on my hands but not on my heart." No great cause can be properly served if it is not borne on our hearts. Therein lies the final test of spiritual awakening, that we go into the city where men live and work and play and suffer, and take their problems not only on our hands but also on our hearts.

God forbid that on Easter Day any Christian should be disillusioned about life or disheartened about himself! Christ lived to empower us, to challenge us, and to change our selfish inertia into radiant and sacrificial service. He came not to lull us to sleep with an easy optimism but to stab us awake with a costly realism. He rang God's bell! May each of us this day of resurrection actually begin a new life, a life that will go into the city and change it, that will appear unto many and win them, that will surge in upon us and fill us with a zest for high adventure with Christ. "The saints who had fallen asleep arose!"

9

CAN WE BELIEVE IN ETERNAL LIFE?

by WILLIAM E. HULME

Professor, Wartburg Theological Seminary,
Dubuque, Iowa

"Because I live, ye shall live also."
—JOHN 14:19b

"BECAUSE I live, ye shall live also." Christ has risen from the dead! Hallelujah! Because he lives—and here is our joy and hope in Easter—we too shall live, live beyond the grave, live forever!

As soon as we say this, we begin the battle with doubt. Oh, perhaps not so much on Easter Sunday. The excitement of that first Easter is in the air. "Now upon the first day of the week, very early in the morning"—so begins the thrilling account, told in exciting style, as the narrators relived the experiences of that first Easter. You share the depression of Mary Magdalene, Salome and Mary the mother of James as they walk to the tomb of their crucified master. You gasp with them as they look within the tomb and see not the body but the angels. You thrill with Mary Magdalene as she realizes through her tears that the man she thought to be the gardener was the risen Lord himself. "Master," she cried, and all her hopes were born again.

But after the celebration is over—then the haunting question, is it really true? Ours is not an easy age in which to believe in a resurrection from the dead. This is the age

CAN WE BELIEVE IN ETERNAL LIFE?

of science. Without even being conscious of it we think scientifically. Death has all the earmarks of being final. How can that which is dead—really dead—live again? As Christians, it disturbs us even to raise the question. It is all too threatening. Humanly speaking the evidence seems to be on the other side. "For the fate of the sons of men and the fate of beasts is the same; as one dies, so dies the other."

And yet through twenty centuries of uninterrupted witness the Christian church has testified to the reality of a resurrection. The church came into existence because those early followers of Jesus believed with all their hearts that they witnessed the risen Christ, and they bore their witness to the world with enthusiasm and with power. In the words of Charles Clayton Morrison, "The early church grew from eleven men to tens of thousands in the first generation after Christ because it conquered death—the final enemy of every living soul."

But even the church has not escaped the influence of our scientific age. The church is not talking much these days about death and the life beyond. We believe in a *this*-worldly religion. Let's worry about living—not dying! Even secular professions have noticed the change. A member of the faculty of the New York Psychoanalytic Institute has written a book entitled, *The Psychiatrist and the Dying Patient*. In it he says that belief in any afterlife has declined to a point that it is of little value to the psychiatrist. Therefore the need of the dying patient is to be kept unaware of his approaching death. Death, of course, is senseless. But so, he says, is life.

Religiously speaking he has a point. If death is senseless, so also is life. Yet what are we going to say to our age about death? Our quietness merely reflects the common resistance of our day to talk about death.

But there is another side to our quietness. <u>We are rebelling against an otherworldly emphasis in the church of a previous day.</u> In rummaging through some old books I found a religious book for children that belonged to my father when he was a child. It was hard to believe that such material could have been printed—so different was this time from ours. Almost every story in some way or other dealt with dying and going to heaven. Usually the story was about some little child who was dying. As the family gathered about the bedside the dying youngster gave an angelic farewell and fondly looked forward to the heavenly mansions.

Now we hardly even mention death in children's religious literature. Again our age of science has had something to do with this change. The tremendous advance in medical science has made death a rare rather than a common occurrence in childhood. It is easier in our day to dismiss the subject of death than it once was. It is also easier to dismiss the old emphasis on the next world as the answer to the problems of this world. We can see this change, for example, in the way we sing the table prayer, "Be present at our table, Lord." Where we used to be content to sing the last line as, "may feast in paradise with thee" we now prefer to change it to, "may strengthened for thy service be."

Even when we talk about eternal life we prefer to emphasize the fact that eternal life is a present reality. It is a quality of living rather than a future kind of existence. If our older emphasis on the other world was an escape from facing the problems of life, our present emphasis on this world is also an escape. If one was an escape from life, the other is an escape from death. And if it is true that in the midst of life we are in death, then a this-worldly emphasis is also an escape from life.

CAN WE BELIEVE IN ETERNAL LIFE?

At the Lutheran World Federation Assembly at Minneapolis, Bishop Krummacher of East Germany gave an address that made quite a few of us uncomfortable. Instead of talking about how Christianity can improve our living in *this* world, he talked about the hope of victory when Christ would return to establish his kingdom. This was so different from what we had been hearing! What other hope could a leader of the church have in a Communist satellite state? Of what value to him is a this-worldly Christianity that is best known for its ability to relieve us of our psychic pains, to help us enjoy life, to get along with our family, and to bring success to our endeavors? People in the Iron Curtain countries know far better than we what St. Paul meant when he said, "If in this life only we have hope in Christ, we are of all men most miserable." To talk about eternal life as something that we experience here and now is fine and good, but what about the future—a future that must include death?

Can we still believe today in life that goes beyond the grave? Before we dare answer such a question we will have to ask ourselves why we are even interested in asking it. Perhaps you think this is a silly thing to say. Who but a dismal person would like the idea of going out of existence? Is not this at least one reason why we fear death—that it threatens to bring an end to us? And who wants to end? No doubt about it—the desire to survive the experience of death is quite universal. But it is not a particularly Christian desire.

Over and beyond the mere desire for survival, do we not all desire to see our departed loved ones again? In fact is this not the hope the church often holds out to the bereaved? And is it not normal and natural that we be interested in the life beyond for this reason? It is normal, but it still is not a particularly Christian reason.

WILLIAM E. HULME

Immanuel Kant said that nobody has the right to talk about immortality until he has worked so hard at being mortal that he longs for the immortal. I am not sure I know all that Kant meant by this, but I think that the Apostle Paul is a good example of it. After a long and devoted career as an ambassador for Christ he was arrested and put in a Roman prison. Not knowing what the future held in store for him, he had the one hope that Christ would be honored in his body, whether by life or death. But as to which of the two he desired—life or death—he could not tell. On the one hand he had an honest longing to depart this life and be with Christ, which, he said, was far better. But to remain in this life was more important to the people whom he served. Convinced of this he desired to remain, so that they would have ample cause to glory in Jesus Christ when he returned to them. Here was a longing for the other world that surely was no escape. If anything it was a real incentive to go to work in this world.

The Christian longing for eternal life comes out of an identification with Christ and his cause. Here we have no lasting city—our world is not the kingdom of God—but we seek one to come. The Christian hope for the future is for the victory of Jesus Christ—when "the kingdoms of this world are become the kingdoms of our Lord, and of his Christ, and he shall reign forever and ever." The more we work to bring this victory to pass now, the more the eternal hope will grow on us. The more we hunger and thirst after righteousness now, the more we shall long for that day when we shall be able to love the Lord our God with all our heart and our neighbor as ourself. The more we bear the cross that goes with being a Christian, the more our belief in the resurrection will become firm and sure.

CAN WE BELIEVE IN ETERNAL LIFE?

This kind of belief does not come by scientific proof. Even if the resurrection of Jesus could be established as a scientific fact, it would not on this account change people's lives. Our Lord himself said this very thing. In his parable of the rich man and Lazarus he told how Lazarus in this life had nothing, while the rich man had everything. When Lazarus died he was carried by the angels into heaven to be with Abraham. The rich man also died but he went to hell. Being in torment he looked across the great chasm and saw Lazarus resting in Abraham's bosom. After he realized he could get no relief for himself, he called out to Abraham, "I beg you, father, to send Lazarus to my father's house, for I have five brothers, so that he may warn them, lest they also come into this place of torment, for if someone goes to them from the dead, they will repent."

But Abraham said to him, "If they do not hear Moses and the prophets—that is, the Scripture—neither will they be convinced if someone should rise from the dead." It is not scientific proof that changes personality; it is faith.

Believing as he did, we would not expect the risen Lord to show himself alive to those who had crucified him. He was not interested in forcing people to accept a fact. Rather he was interested in encouraging people to believe in the kingdom of God. So he showed himself to those who had shown an interest beforehand. When one of his disciples demanded scientific proof, Jesus gave it to him. But then he said, "Have you believed because you have seen me, Thomas? Blessed are those who have not seen and yet believe."

Can we believe in a resurrection from the dead? Only if we seek the evidence where it alone can be found—in the realm of faith. It is as we follow him in life that we can believe in him in death. It is through what we know about him now that we are able to trust in him in the face of something so impenetrable as death.

Every venture in faith is a leap into the unknown. When we believe in God we are inspired not only to leap but to leap in confidence. Death calls for the biggest leap of all. It is the experience that comes from the lesser leaps that gives us hope for the big leap. The faith that can bridge the chasm of death with the sure and certain hope of the resurrection is the same faith that day after day enlightens our life through a very real and meaningful fellowship with God.

And what a hope we have! The New Testament abounds in pictures and symbols that attempt to describe the magnificence of the life to come. But in the last analysis it is too much even for pictures and symbols. For "eye hath not seen, nor ear heard, neither have entered into the heart of man, the things which God hath prepared for them that love him. But God hath revealed them unto us by his Spirit." In the fellowship of faith we get a glimpse—an anticipation—of the glory ahead, the city yet to come.

With this kind of a hope for the future, let us throw ourselves into the business of living in the present. Shoulder to shoulder with the risen Christ and our fellow believers, let us work for the kingdom of God while there is yet time—buoyed up with the confidence that despite whatever setbacks we may have, the cause of righteousness will finally triumph. God's victory shall be complete and I—here is the Christian hope—I shall participate in it. For we are "fellow heirs with Christ."

Christ is risen! His victory is our victory! His resurrection is our resurrection. "Because he lives, we shall live also." "I believe in the resurrection of the body and the life everlasting." Hallelujah!

10

THE QUESTION, THE CANDLE, THE ARROW

by GERALD KENNEDY

Bishop, The Methodist Church, Los Angeles Area, Los Angeles, California

". . . that I may know him and the power of his resurrection, and may share his sufferings, becoming like him in death, that if possible I may attain the resurrection from the dead."
—PHILIPPIANS 3:10-11

SOMEWHERE I read of a Bible study method developed in Sweden. A leader reads aloud a passage of Scripture to the group, and then each member considers the passage by himself and meditates upon it. Where there is a word or a phrase or a verse that is not clear, the person places a question mark in the margin. The phrase or sentence that begins to throw light on the text has a candle placed opposite it. Finally, the word or verse that strikes the conscience with a demand, is marked with an arrow.

There is a sense in which this is the way truth always finds us. First there is the question and the mystery. Slowly it begins to shine in its own light or is illumined by other facts and experience. Finally it strikes home to our own being with a demand for a decision or an adjustment of our thinking. So the resurrection, this central affirmation of the Christian faith, comes to us as a question, a candle, an arrow.

GERALD KENNEDY

First of all, then, let us consider the Easter experience as a question mark.

<u>We ought not to forget that what drew the women to the tomb on that first Easter morning was not hope, but despair.</u> It was not assurance, it was disappointment. In their unhappiness they had to do something and so they decided they could at least anoint with spices the dead body of the one they loved. There was simply nothing else they could do. But they went to the burial place of Jesus with sadness and not with expectancy.

This is the mood that best describes our time. We are in the midst of much confusion. I hesitate to confess that I like to look at Westerns on TV, but a Stanford professor who confessed to a like weakness analysed the reasons which fit my situation. He said it was a relief to look at a simple world where wrong was black and right was white. Above all, he found it a relief to believe that evil could be destroyed with a six-shooter. I wonder if the great appeal of Westerns is to our unconscious desire for escape from a confusion that becomes at times almost unbearable. We long for a simpler world.

The world seems hopelessly complex. Who has a simple answer to the problems that haunt every waking moment? Where are the easy rules of happiness and who can tell us how to live calmly and wisely? Who is able to find the pattern of nobility in this conglomeration of seemingly unrelated events? Goodness and evil will not separate themselves clearly and a man's destiny seems inextricably interwoven into a dozen designs not of his choosing. John Wanamaker said, "I know half the money I spend on advertising is wasted, but I can never find out which half." So we could confess that much we do is wasted and unprofitable. But which part is wasted?

Yet we cannot accept this confusion as the ultimate

THE QUESTION, THE CANDLE, THE ARROW

condition of life. We cannot believe that this is the inevitable situation. Somewhere there must be a clue and somewhere it must be possible to discover the meaning of it all. One of the mysteries of human life is man's inability to escape the sense of meaning in life. As Professor Edwin Conklin, biologist of Princeton University, has said, "The probability of life originating from accident is comparable to the probability of the Unabridged Dictionary resulting from an explosion in a printing shop."

Yet no matter how far we go in our knowledge we merely enlarge the realm of mystery. Each expansion of the light reveals an even greater extension of the darkness. It is true as the Nineteenth Century scientist phrased it, that we are at best merely children playing with some shells on the beach while the ocean extends out beyond us in all its vastness. For finally, we are confronted with death. Whatever little success we may have in exploring our environment on the earth, we cannot penetrate beyond our dying with anything like scientific knowledge. So we are forever faced with the question mark.

At a public meeting that was badly out of hand, the room was full of noisy, conflicting voices, all trying to make themselves heard. Finally the chairman rapped sharply with his gavel and called out loudly, "Gentlemen, gentlemen! Please let us keep this confusion orderly." So we cry out for some orderliness in the midst of our confusion. Over our minds as we are confronted with life, there ever looms the question mark of death.

In the second place, the resurrection experience comes to us as a candle.

The passing centuries make the event shine with an ever-increasing brilliance. It has stood through all the testing of time and cynical attack. The darkness has never been able to put it out.

The resurrection is an illumination of the nature of God. It reveals him as austere and stern. He is no uncle wanting the young people to have a good time while the parents deal with the more serious matters of training and discipline. He is the Father who puts high demands upon his children because he loves them. There is nothing sentimental about the God who emerges from the shadows into the light of the resurrection.

The atonement is not for his sake but for ours. He is no tribal chieftain demanding payment for a broken custom. He is no helpless potentate caught in his own network of legislation. He is the God revealed as love that brings forgiveness and redemption. God stands forth in this light as utterly dependable who will find us in our worst and through suffering bring us to triumph.

John Bunyan in *Grace Abounding to the Chief of Sinners* describes a period of deep personal depression in the year 1652. Suddenly there fell upon his mind a word of hope: "Look at the generations of old, and see: Did ever any trust in the Lord and was confounded?" He says that this greatly lightened his spirit and he searched for the text until he found it finally, in the apocryphal book of Ecclesiasticus. So the resurrection has lightened the spirits of men through the ages with this revelation of God's dependability and concern.

Here is light for the understanding of man's nature. We are made for greatness, not for littleness. We are created for fellowship with God, and we are made for eternity. The clue to human nature is not to be found in the jungle ethics of our contemporaries or in the cheap and tawdry behavior of so many of our heroes. It is to be found in Jesus Christ who went to the Cross and was raised on the third day by God.

Man can become an exploiter and a seeker after the

THE QUESTION, THE CANDLE, THE ARROW

main chance. That this is true of many men, cannot be denied by any explorer of his own heart. But what man is meant to be, is best revealed through testimony such as that of Adlai Stevenson, regarding the missionaries of Africa. This is his tribute:

"Anyone who travels there is constantly reminded of their heroism. Missionaries laid a groundwork in religion, health and education under difficult and dangerous circumstances. What they have done is almost beyond belief. They fought yellow fever, dysentery, parasites. And the gravestones I saw! My God, their gravestones—all through Africa." [1]

This is human nature at its best and it finds its inspiration in Christ.

In the resurrection, there is the revelation of life. Our life is not a cheap romance or a silly yarn such as are found on magazine shelves in a bus depot. Since Jesus lived and died, we cannot think of man's life as a mere tale told by some idiot with no more than a passing interest. It is indeed a mighty epic, full of the grandeur of the eternal. It is full of tragedy, nobility, virtue. It is a facing of great issues and a business with God.

Sometime ago, that great counselor of youth, Zsa Zsa Gabor, uttered an oracle on the subject of love. "Marriage," she observed, "does something to a love affair, takes something out of it. There is a piquancy about love when two people know they can leave one another that never exists inside the circle of the wedding ring." Halford Luccock commented on this and reminded us of a remark made by John Strachey concerning Winston Churchill's biography of the Duke of Marlborough. Speaking of the life-long devotion of the Duke and his wife to each other,

[1] *Christian Century,* Oct. 9, 1957

Strachey said, "Such a story of married love makes all the sizzling pictures of Purple Passions, served up on the newsstands, taste like ten cents worth of cold potatoes." Amen!

So much of our modern life tastes like ten cents worth of cold potatoes! So much of the talk we hear sounds dull and wearisome. So much of our glitter lasts but a moment and then the darkness descends more frightening than before. But to every generation, there comes the Easter experience to light a candle of hope and power in the midst of our darkness.

Finally, the resurrection is an arrow—which is to say that here is something we cannot escape. To treat it as an isolated event we may take or leave, is to misunderstand it completely. It is one of those cosmic happenings which has absolute meaning. If it is true, it has terrible and wonderful implications for each man's life. If it is true, and I try to ignore it, I shall be found by its truth when it is too late. In any case, we are faced on Easter with something inescapable.

In all kindness, we must speak to the people who give it a passing nod once a year. The Easter Sunday Christians, like the poor, we have always with us. Yet their attitude is suicidal and deadly. For, mark you, if Easter is true, then my denying it makes all my life a lie. If it is not true, then as Paul said, "we are of all men most to be pitied." Nothing more for us is left but stoicism and unfortunately, most of us are not up to that lofty, lonely comfortless ethic. We have to come to terms with death and what we believe about it. For that is the ultimate experience that casts its influence on every human activity.

What must we do now? What did the women do at the empty tomb? They bore witness to something that changed their lives and formed the basis for eternal hope. They became instruments of a power that overcame the

THE QUESTION, THE CANDLE, THE ARROW

world, even the Christian faith. It was not merely an artificial pumping up of enthusiasm or excitement, but a release of light and energy.

At the decisive naval battle of Trafalgar, a signal was run up on the Admiral's ship just before the ships closed on each other. It read: "England expects every man will do his duty." Collingwood saw the signal and remarked testily, "I wish Nelson would stop signalling, as we all know well enough what we have to do." But the message brought cheers from the ships in his line. Once the arrow of the resurrection has found us, we do not need to be told what we must do about our living. But every time we think of it, our hearts are lifted up with rejoicing.

At last we commit ourselves to this event. You see, the only way to make a valid test is to assume, for the time being at least, that the hypothesis is true. This applies to science as well as to religion. We test a thing by acting upon it. Either it works or its does not, but we shall only know after we have ventured forth in faith. This, I take it, is what Paul is saying to us in the text. We live the truth of the resurrection and then we find its power. This mighty experience is shared by Christ. We find that we are raised to new life here and now. Until the doctrine of life eternal becomes to us a living reality, it has not fulfilled its meaning.

Facing the wonder and glory of this experience of hope and assurance, we know ourselves to be the recipients of a gift beyond our imagining. We are like the writers who long for publication and finally go to some "vanity press" that we may have our names in a book. Why is this so important? The editor of one such publishing firm sums it up in these words: "Other houses may promise riches . . . we just offer immortality." And that is more important than riches.

GERALD KENNEDY

When the question mark becomes a candle, and the candle becomes an arrow, then the resurrection experience is complete for us. Then we want to sing in the words of a hymn so popular with great revival crowds across America:

> O Lord my God, when I in awesome wonder
> Consider all the worlds Thy hands have made,
> And see the stars, and hear the rolling thunder,
> Thy power throughout the universe displayed—
> Then sings my soul, my Savior God, to Thee:
> How great Thou art, how great Thou art!

11

WORDS OF THE RISEN LORD

by A. R. KRETZMANN

Pastor, St. Luke's Lutheran Church, Chicago, Illinois

ALL Easter stories begin with tears and darkness and the sealed-up tomb. It takes awhile before the vision of angels, the frightened guards, and the risen One begin to dawn upon our consciousness. We are confronted now with the risen Christ—the all-knowing one—who knew the agony of the pre-Easter days. For him, Gethsemane and Golgotha were not mere words and not mere history, as they have been for millions since that day. For him they were the agony of the denials and of damnings; of prayers and pains; of loss and labor. There were some wonders from the side of God—the black sky, the rent rocks, the centurion's confession, the love of the women, and the courage of Joseph and Nicodemus. And now, angels—angels to proclaim that he has risen; guards to flee frightened into the city; Peter and John to run swiftly to the grave; and the Marys, with their sorrows and their ointments, come to make a decent burial out of an execution.

By the glory of him, Mary became the first evangelist of the resurrection. As Luther says, "The Lord himself makes a preacher of her. She shall teach the apostles." Note how the fear of loneliness and loss is suddenly gone when our Lord says to Mary, "Woman, why weepest thou? Whom seekest thou?" This he could have said to anyone, but then he makes true what Isaiah said: "I have called thee by thy name, thou art mine." Jesus saith unto her, "Mary." She turned herself, and said unto him, "Master." Truly he was "Master" now—Lord of life and death, returned from hell and the grave. "Weeping may endure for a night but joy cometh in the morning." The first word of Christ is a word to a single soul in need of help.

"Ought not Christ to have suffered these things, and to enter into his glory?"

Even when the fears of loneliness and loss have been answered, we still come burdened with the fear of suffering, particularly of our loved one. Here were the two men on the Emmaus road, witnesses of the greatest events in the history of mankind, watching the opening of the gates of mercy for all men, seeing the curtains of the old law torn away and a new light dawning over the earth. And all the while, says the Scripture, "their eyes were held."

On the afternoon of the first Easter Day Christ joins them as they are leaving Jerusalem. He listens to what they have to say and then begins to show how Moses and all the prophets spoke of him—how the Holy Scripture has no meaning without him.

What passages could he have discussed with the men on the road? Was it Psalm 16, "Thou wilt not leave my soul in hell; neither wilt thou suffer thine holy one to see corruption?" Was it Psalm 8, "Thou hast made him a little lower than the angels, and hast crowned him with glory and majesty?" Was it Psalm 110, "The Lord said unto my Lord, Sit thou at my right hand, until I make thine enemies my footstool?" Was it Isaiah 53, **"Surely** he hath born our griefs and carried our sorrows. . . . **He** was wounded for our transgressions, he was bruised for

WORDS OF THE RISEN LORD

our iniquities: the chastisement of our peace was upon him; and with his stripes we are healed. . . ."?

You can go on in endless lines to bind together all the great prophecies of the Old Testament and all the fulfillment of the New. Here you find the risen One himself lifting the veil. This exposition of Christ is as great a miracle as the resurrection itself. This certifies that all—the suffering, the death, the resurrection, everything—was in the plan of God, and in the love of God, and in the goodness of God.

The disciples treat our Lord as though he were to be their guest. We forget how much we need to be *his* guests. We feed on the straw and husks because we will not follow where he bids us come. Our souls go starving on their dreary way because we have not sense enough to know that Christ must rise and live and be the Bread of Life for *us*.

The first word has been a single word for one; the second word for two and now the third for those who were disciples of our Lord!

"Peace be unto you. Why are ye troubled? Why do thoughts arise in your hearts? Behold my hands and my feet, that it is I myself: handle me and see; for a spirit hath not flesh and bones, as ye see me have."

Along with the fear of loneliness and the fear of the suffering of our loved ones comes the fear of disillusionment. What if all this were only a dream? What if the disillusioners have gained their point and show that all our Lord's appearance was only a spirit? That is why our Lord holds forth his hands with nail prints in them, and shows his feet with unhealed wounds and bares his side that they may see that this is body and blood, and flesh and bones, of him who died upon the Cross.

This was something so startling and new that the frightened disciples must be calmed by his words, "Peace be unto you." Mysteriously he had appeared in their midst and just as mysteriously he would be gone again. So he comes to our lives too and speaks his word of peace. He is everywhere according to his will. He enters in where no one sees him come, or go, and yet he has the true body and blood of a true child of man. With this word of Christ a whole new world began. Bodies moldering away in the earth these many years shall rise again in likeness of his glorified body. Never weaken in your faith about the new life! It is not only the assurance that all our sins are forgiven but also that he who forgave them in his death on the Cross now lives eternally, and we shall live with him.

Now after the first three fears there comes a fourth. Thomas, the outspoken doubter, must have his answer and his way:

"Thomas reach hither thy finger, and behold my hands; and thrust it into my side: and be not faithless, but believing. . . . Blessed are they that have not seen, and yet have believed."

Thomas is not sure. He is afraid of what he cannot comprehend. He will believe only what he sees himself. The testimony of ten other apostles, and two other women, and the disciples of the Emmaus road, means nothing to him. "Except I put my fingers into the nail prints in his hands and thrust my hand into his side, I will not believe." He does not mean that he doubts the fact that they have seen the Lord. He wants to see him too, but when he sees him he will demand the support of his sense of touch—the wounds shall be the final evidence.

It is a wonderful condescension on the part of our Lord

WORDS OF THE RISEN LORD

that he comes to doubters like Thomas and all of us. The doubter who declared war on the risen One is greeted by the gentle word, "Peace be unto you." Jesus not only speaks the words but he brings peace in himself for he presents the wounds and the open side to wipe away forever the doubts of Thomas.

Almost at once Thomas is on his knees before his Lord. Out of the very depths of his being he utters the cry of faith and recognition, "My Lord and my God." Until this time no one had so clearly discerned and expressed the great enigma of Jesus Christ. The resurrected One makes Thomas the great teacher of the church which would repeat his confession over and over again throughout the long centuries. "I believe in one Lord Jesus Christ, the only begotten Son of God. . . ."

We learned it all from Thomas, and Thomas learned it from his Lord. The reality of the resurrection and the witness of the resurrection is all the same. Christ brings us this in order that we might not hang on things like seeing, or the evidence of our senses, when we have the evidence of our Savior. The blessing is not for Thomas, for Thomas believed only because he saw. The blessing did not even count for the disciples, for the Lord appeared to them. The blessing is for us and all the multitudes who never saw him after his ascension, but truly believed. When, therefore, we think this Easter Day, "Oh, that I had lived in yonder, blessed time and seen my Lord himself," then we should be reminded, "Blessed are they that have not seen and yet have believed."

To the other fears man would also add the fear of rejection. This was the lingering fear as Peter meets his risen Lord on the shores of the Sea of Galilee:

A. R. KRETZMANN

"Simon, son of Jonas, lovest thou me more than these?"

Peter had every reason to believe that he would be rejected. He had promised to be faithful, and he had denied his Lord with cursing. He had promised to go into death with him, and he had run away to hide behind locked doors. He had promised to be faithful even if all others forsook him.

Our Lord comes to us in the same way. Always we fear rejection; always we feel unworthy; never does he rake up the past, but always he looks to the future and says, "Behold I make all things new."

"Do you love me now? . . . Do you love me now, Simon Barjona? . . . Do you love me more than these?" The threefold request for love now, reminds us of the threefold denial in the past. The threefold profession of love puts him into office again—the threefold ordination to the pastoral office, the service of a shepherd.

That is the way our Lord dealt with all those who saw him after his resurrection. There were no reproaches for their denials, nor any criticism of their flight. There was only a holy ordination and commission to go and do something now with the glory of the Cross and the miracle of the resurrection.

Then listen as our Lord makes life come alive with purpose and peace:

"Peace be unto you: as my Father hath sent me, even so send I you."

Who was it whom the Father had sent? His only begotten Son—"Begotten of His Father before all worlds, God of God, Light of Light, Very God of very God, Begotten not made, being of one substance with the Father."

Whom does the Son send? Mere creatures, who have

WORDS OF THE RISEN LORD

their beginnings in time and their end in time—who are always opposed to the good and the holy—who rebel in disobedience against the Father and the Son, their Creator and Redeemer.

When the Son was sent by the Father it meant that God deprived him of the joys of heaven and made him to be sin for us who knew no sin. When the Son sends mere creatures this is a vocation. But when they respond to God's love in Christ, the children of wrath become the children of love. The sinners become the sinless, and the far-off are brought near. God is now the Father of love and light, who is always with us, and through us calls others to his love and mercy. Ordinary men become great apostles, messengers of God, and brothers of Christ.

The man of "no purpose" will always excuse himself by saying that he is the man of no power. But God has an answer for that:

"Receive ye the Holy Ghost: Whose soever sins ye remit, they are remitted unto them; and whose soever sins ye retain, they are retained."

You see now how God remakes a man when the resurrected One becomes real in his life! The word which is used here for "the Lord Jesus *'breathed'* on his disciples," is the equivalent word which is used in Genesis for the creation of man, "And God *breathed* into his nostrils a living soul." This is the word which is used when Ezekiel sees the vision of the dead men's bones come alive.

So this "breath of life" comes to the disciples. The sending of sinners as ambassadors for Christ is no less important than God breathing life into the first man. This "sending forth" is creation and resurrection from the dead. The waiting apostles in Jerusalem are really waiting for their Lord to take hold of them. When men are seized by the triune God they become messengers in the name of that God.

They will need his blessing for he sends them out into peacelessness, and restlessness, and homelessness. God be with you now that you have power!

"All power is given unto me in heaven and in earth."

A man might feel that he was very strong but that he lacked both leadership and direction. Our Lord supplies them both. He leads the way to genuine power. What a challenge that was for this little band! Only eleven people without money, without weapons, without friends, without knowledge of new languages, without any special gifts of speech or mind. He tells them to hold fast to whatever he shall command them. Caesars and Herods would rage against them. Jew, Greek, Roman, and a thousand others would persecute them, but he would be with them.

"Lo, I am with you always, even unto the end of the world."

This is the word that Christ gives to his chosen men. So shall they work on the nations of the world. So he sends forth his great ambassadors, and says that he will be with them wherever they go. His physical appearances stop now. He does not appear just here and there in the Holy Land but now he is always and everywhere among all his people. Now we no longer need to have to wait for an appearance on his part, because he is always, and everywhere, in the midst of those who call upon him and glorify his name. And if this communion is even now so strong and so good, just think what it will be when he returns again, and makes an end of all that is the world, and we shall see him face to face.

What are you going to do in the meantime with the glory of the resurrection? He tells us very clearly.

"Go ye into all the world, and preach the Gospel to every creature. He that believeth and is baptized shall be saved; but he that believeth not shall be damned."

The judgment begins even now! Wherever the word of God is preached there the judgment begins. He who believes in this Christ revealed in the Gospel has eternal life. "He that believeth in him is not come into judgment, but whosoever believeth not is judged because he believeth not on the name of the only begotten Son of God." In other words, the preaching of the Gospel is the decision between life and death even now. You cannot ignore it! "He that believeth and is baptized" is already received with Christ . . . the believers are already a new creation, "The old is passed away, behold all things are new."

What a tremendous responsibility to put upon our preaching, our going to church, our hearing of the Word of God—on this new day of the resurrection!

12

CHRIST BREAKS THROUGH

by DAVID A. MacLENNAN

Pastor, Brick Presbyterian Church, Rochester, New York

"and he rolled a stone against the door of the tomb."

—MARK 15:46

"When the doors were shut where the disciples were assembled for fear . . . came Jesus and stood in the midst, and saith unto them, Peace be unto you." (Ronald Knox translation: *"The disciples had locked the doors of the room in which they had assembled: and Jesus came, and stood there in their midst: Peace be upon you, He said."*)

—JOHN 20:19

History's greatest drama has God for author and chief actor. It is a divine-human drama with cosmic background and for stage this familiar earth. View it in three acts: Barrier, Defeat, Break-through.

ACT I. THE BARRIER

"And he rolled a stone against the door of the tomb." A sombre note of finality is struck by such a sentence. It occurs in our earliest Gospel report of the burial of Jesus' body. Joseph of Arimathea, respected member of the council and a secret follower of Jesus, risked his career and possibly his life by boldly asking the Roman governor

CHRIST BREAKS THROUGH

for the custody of the body. The councilor wanted to give it a decent burial in his own newly-hewn rock tomb. Pilate sent for the army officer commanding the execution detail, learned how long Jesus had been dead, and gave permission to Joseph to conduct the funeral. After taking the body down from the Cross and wrapping it in a linen winding sheet, he put Jesus in the tomb. "And he rolled a stone against the door of the tomb." Physical death seems the ultimate insuperable barrier.

If you have ever been present at the interment of the body of a loved person, you know how the modern equivalent of what Joseph did suggests the end with shocking vividness. "When archaeologists began to excavate Roman cemeteries, they discovered that nearly all the grave markers had seven letters carved on them— N F F NS NC. These are the first letters of the words in four brief sentences—sentences so familiar to the Roman world that the bare initials of the words were sufficient for their identification. The sentences were these: 'Non fui.' 'Fui.' 'Non sum.' 'Non curo.' 'I was not.' 'I was.' 'I am not.' 'I do not care.' "

The mood of those four sentences expresses fatalistic surrender to the finality of physical death. Under the chill of that surrender the ancient world lived. Under it many moderns live. Some of them are the finest persons. They cannot see how the Easter story can be true. They cannot see how personality survives bodily death. They may even come to church at Easter, hoping to be convinced despite their doubts.

Are the seven letters which were found on Roman grave markers also carved on Joseph of Arimathea's tomb? "And he rolled a stone against the door of the tomb."

Did you ever wonder what happened to the people who

participated in the grim drama of Good Friday? On the Friday night? On the Saturday?

ACT II. DEFEAT

The crowd went home. Many of them had yelled for Jesus' death. Mobs easily become subhuman and easy to manipulate by determined plotters. Many were simply spectators. Crowds always disperse.

Caiaphas and Annas, the ecclesiastics who had plotted the crime, must have experienced deep self-satisfaction. They were preservers of the status quo and they had succeeded in preserving it. That Nazarene troublemaker was out of the way.

The money makers went back to the Temple and resumed their profitable business of trading. "Business as usual" is sound sense in time of revolution or recession.

As for the Governor, doubtless Pontius Pilate remained uneasy for quite a while. He had played his part with reluctance. But now, perhaps he could "rest easy." At least Rome would receive no more reports of disturbances in this hot spot of resistance to imperial rule. He sent a squad of troops to guard the tomb. As my friend, Professor James A. Sanders suggests, he may have ordered one of the household staff: "Be sure to wash that basin I used at the railing before the mob. If there's one thing I can't stand it's a dirty basin."

What did Barabbas do? He was the prisoner who won the reprieve denied Jesus. He may have watched the Man die in his place. On that black Friday night he might have celebrated his "lucky break." It could be that Barabbas made a private pilgrimage to the tomb, stood a moment or two in front of the stone door sealing the entrance, saying to himself, "By right I should be on the other side of that stone." Par Lagerkvist wrote his novel

CHRIST BREAKS THROUGH

Barabbas to indicate how Jesus' death haunted the pardoned criminal to the end of his road.

Judas Iscariot? What happened to him? What happened *in* him that made him swing between earth and sky?

The disciples? Could they ever forget that they "all forsook him and fled" when the sullen soldiers laid violent hands on their master, flashed their torchlights into their faces? "We ran. Even when we knew that our cause was lost we could have stayed by him to the end. Well, the cause *is* lost. We saw it nailed to that cursed tree with him." Soon, one by one, they took their way back to the Upper Room. The chalice still stood on the table. As they sat there, dejected, defeated, some of them a little afraid, those wonderful words he spoke during their last meal together came back. They seemed to echo from the ceiling and walls. "Let not your heart be troubled. Believe in God. Believe also in me. Peace I leave with you. . . . A new commandment I give unto you that you love one another." The commandment day—the mandate anniversary—Maundy Thursday, the anniversary would be called long afterward. "You are my friends if you do whatsoever I command you. It is expedient for you that I go away. And if I go away, I will come again . . ."

One, and then another, would get up, with pain in his eyes. "I can't stand it. I'm going away. I'm going home . . . I'm going to try fishing again." Some would walk swiftly to the tomb again. The stone is still there.

What of the women who had followed him so long? They remained watching him die. Good women remain loyal longer than most men. They mourn their dearest longer. The women who followed Jesus and meant so much to him prepared spices and ointments. But their hearts were like lead. The skies were darkened. They shuddered at the flashback of the events of Friday. "And God didn't lift a finger to help him! Let's not go on with the work . . ."

So the best and the worst of men and women felt that spiritual faith was a fraud. You might have heard them say: "Goodness and mercy don't follow us or anyone else all the days of our life. We don't dwell in God's house forever . . . and you don't walk *through* the valley of the shadow of death."

They really believed that all was lost, that the hopes, the promises, the dreams are false. The assurance that life and love shall reign forever when the worlds lie dead is fantasy, illusion, a lie.

Life rolls stones, seals tombs, buries hope, nails dreams to hard wood. Bitter disappointment, defeat, frustration, sickness, death: these make life. Yes, there are interludes of happiness and relative peace—if you're lucky. But always there is a Cross against the sky. Truth is forever on a scaffold. Wrong is on a throne. It looked like that to Peter, to all the disciples and to the women, too. It would have looked that black to us had we been living then. But we are living now.

ACT III. BREAK-THROUGH

Christ broke through the tomb, broke through the final barricade of bodily death.

Does this mean that to accept the foundation-belief of the Christian faith you must believe in the resurrection of the physical body of Christ? I cannot think that believing that restoration of the actual flesh and blood of Christ's physical body is essential to belief in the resurrection of Christ. Concerning ordinary human beings, I am in good company when I do not believe in physical resurrection, if by that you mean a belief "that the actual particles of a man's body are gathered together after death and reassembled."

Nevertheless, I most certainly believe in the resurrection of the Lord Jesus Christ. I am convinced that his body was not spirited away by his disciples. All Jesus' enemies had to do to disprove the incredible claim of the first followers was to produce the lifeless body of Jesus. Nor can I believe that Jesus only swooned, and that in the cool of the tomb he recovered and made his way out. Romans took special care to see that criminals condemned to be executed were in fact dead. Moreover, it is absurd to think that the disciples "who were hiding in terror, stole the body of Jesus, disposed of it, and then suddenly became heroes and martyrs, ready to preach the gospel of the resurrection, to die for the truth of a story they made up for themselves, and to inaugurate a movement to teach men truth by founding it on a lie," as Leslie Weatherhead says.

But we are left facing the question, "What happened to the body?" I do not know. It may be that the scientific view of the nature of matter may throw light: "The nature of matter is now regarded as being a form of energy, and whether matter is solid, liquid or gas depends on the speed of the molecules which make it up." Could the mind, the spirit of Christ, act upon his body in such a way as to alter the molecular speed, and make the body into some form of energy which could penetrate stone? Could the molecules be reassembled? It is a mystery, but we do know that mind can radically affect matter.

Here let me use the argument advanced by Dr. Leslie D. Weatherhead in his helpful book, *The Resurrection and the Life*. We cannot say, reasons Dr. Weatherhead, that the resurrection is impossible without knowing everything. To say that it never happened before and that it never happened since is illogical. This is to believe in the closed system theory of the universe. Can you imagine some inhabitant on Mars able to observe earth breaking away from the sun? Everything at first is gaseous, then white-hot, then red-hot. The scenery of the earth must have looked like the inside of a furnace. "Who could possibly have believed that flowers could ever grow . . . that birds could sing and fly in its atmosphere? No one could possibly have predicted the emergence of life on the planet when he looked at an earth that was a glowing furnace. Could anyone before the evolutionary process began have foreseen the arrival of man, the birth of man's consciousness, the power of man to worship, to laugh, to create? But they happened."

But Jesus never appeared as a ghost. "He always got into relationships" with people.

No period was placed at the end of the life of Jesus. It was a comma, a parenthesis. Christ broke through. The grave proved no impassable barrier. God in Christ routed "death's ambuscade." Evil is mighty and on Friday marches as victor invincible. But always the third day comes. God is in charge of his world. "Jesus was crucified, dead and buried." Starkly honest, the church agrees with her enemies and all skeptics. But the church goes on to say, "the third day he rose again from the dead." Easter is not another legend. Here is no cosmic myth. This is the foundation on which the church was built and on which she grows. The God-like love which showed through in Jesus' life is wounded, but not helpless; mortally hurt, but eventually and eternally victorious. Christ broke through. He appeared to men who had hurt him: Peter who denied him, his brother James who sought to restrain

CHRIST BREAKS THROUGH

him; to the chief of the post-Easter opposition, Saul of Tarsus who said, "Last of all, he appeared unto me also."

This is Easter past.

What of Easter present?

Easter is more than the anniversary of V-Day long ago. *It is a present experience of the living Lord.*

God wants us to know that he is alive today.

"I am He that liveth and was dead; and behold, I am alive forevermore."

He is alive in the scriptures.

He is alive in the church. The church is the living organism of which the energy is the spirit of Christ.

He is alive in the worship of the church united with her living Lord.

He is alive in the world. He is at the summit conferences. He is in the valley of the shadow where slavery exists, where tears of bitter failure, hatred and heartbreak reveal broken relationships between individuals and groups.

He lives, not up beyond the clouds, nor in the ionosphere. He lives, but not in stained-glass windows, nor in a kind of racial memory. He shows himself not through psychic investigation but where men and women, boys and girls need him, and are ready to believe where they cannot see.

To live "as if" he were alive and directing us to Christ-like tasks is to know.

One Easter story in the Gospels "finds" me more than any other. It is the one in which Mary has her encounter with the risen Lord. She loved him so much. Quietly he came. He used love's password, "He saith unto her, Mary! She turned herself and said unto him, Master!"

So he comes still . . . Mary! John! Helen! Bill! Jimmy! We know. Christ breaks through, the doors being shut.

13

THE DAY OF THE EARTHQUAKE

by ROY PEARSON

Dean, Andover Newton Theological School,
Newton Centre, Massachusetts

MATTHEW 28:1-9

IT WAS in the spring of the year that it happened. It was in the days when

> . . . the winter is past,
>   the rain is over and gone.
> The flowers appear on the earth,
>   the time of singing has come,
> and the voice of the turtledove
>   is heard in our land.

It was in the spring of the year that it happened, and the world lay hushed and still as the curtain was raised for the greatest drama earth has ever known.

"In the end of the Sabbath . . ." That was how the ancient author opened his story. The Sabbath was the last day of the week. This was the day on which God had rested from his labors in creation, and as the people of the land observed it, the holy hours ran from sunset on Friday to sunset on Saturday. But now the Sabbath was over. Now the sacred day was done.

Yet it was more than a day that was ended in that year of which this story tells. It was an institution, an era, an age. All history would henceforth fall apart at this point,

THE DAY OF THE EARTHQUAKE

and one half of time would lie behind it and the other half would lie ahead. Of course, there was no man on earth who knew that anything unusual had happened as that Sabbath hurried down the fading corridors of the days that are gone, but already the scene on God's stage had been shifted, and the former things were passed away. The end of the Sabbath? Yes, but far more important than that: the end of an epoch, the end of an eon, the end of a world.

"In the end of the Sabbath, *as it began to dawn toward the first day of the week . . ."* The story begins in darkness. If you thought of nothing but the calendar, the Sabbath was over, and the night was gone. The morning had actually come—but not the dawn. Not quite yet. It was perhaps three o'clock on Sunday, and the birds were still asleep in their nests, and the stars were still a pale white in the sky. Black was still earth's color in the land of Palestine, and for the saddened hearts of men the blue and gold of hope were hues of memory but not of expectation.

Yet, all unknown, earth's face was not turned toward the darkness, and just below the eastern hills the chariots of God were speeding toward the dawn. The first day of the week was ready for the earth, and the dawn of that day was like the end of the Sabbath. It was not really a day at all: it was an age, an epoch, a world. And when those hours were over, earth would never be the same again.

But now the action begins, for "in the end of the Sabbath, as it began to dawn toward the first day of the week, *came Mary Magdalene and the other Mary to see the sepulchre."* The first people on the stage are two women. The first people on the stage are trespassers—people who had no right to be there in the garden at all, people who might have been seized if discovered, people who chose the dawn for their visit in the hope of slipping in and out before the city woke from sleep. The first people on the stage are the curious. They did not come to do anything; for there was nothing anyone could do. They did not come to meet the risen Lord; for they did not know that he had risen. They came "to see the sepulchre," to etch upon their memories the place where their Master was buried, and to stand a moment there before this monument to the crucifixion of their hopes and dreams.

"And, behold, there was a great earthquake." Silence, and then uproar. Order, and then tumult. Solitude, and then the awareness of life all around you. Here was the schoolteacher suddenly rapping on her desk for attention. Here was the ship's loudspeaker abruptly blaring into sound with the voice that commands, "Now hear this—." It was as if you were lying asleep in your bed at night, and a pistol were fired beside your ear. It was as if you had rowed your little boat up to a rocky ledge in the ocean and then the "ledge" had moved and you found that you had stepped upon a whale. It was as if God were shaking the earth to compel its awareness. "Wake up!" he was saying. "Wake up, and pay heed! The world is in travail, and a new day is about to be born. Wake up! Wake up!"

"Behold, there was a great earthquake," and what better words could you find to be the prophecy of what was to happen to the world because of that day? This man whose body had been laid in the tomb

> without money and arms, conquered more millions than Alexander, Caesar, Mohammed, and Napoleon; without science and learning, he shed more light on things human and divine than all the philosophers and scholars combined; without the eloquence of the school, he spoke words of life such as were never

spoken before, nor since, and produced effects which lie beyond the reach of orator or poet; without writing a single line, he has set more pens in motion and furnished themes for more sermons, orations, discussions, works of art, learned volumes, and sweet songs of praise than the whole army of great men of ancient and modern times.[1]

An earthquake indeed! An earthquake God-commanded. An earthquake God-inspired.

"For the angel of the Lord descended from heaven, and came and rolled back the stone from the door, and sat upon it." That was what earth always seemed to be doing—putting stones on the pathways of progress, blocking the highroads of redemption, laying man's hopes in a tomb and then sealing the doors against their escape. But now earth had been the ruler long enough. Earth had said enough and done enough. Now it was God's turn, and now God was taking over. So "the angel of the Lord descended from heaven, and came and rolled back the stone from the door." If man could not see what lay behind that stone, God could; and if man would not open the tomb, God would do it himself. Moreover, he would keep it open; for when the angel rolled back the stone from the door, he "sat upon it." There it was, and there it would stay. Christ was loose in the world again, and he would never return to the tomb. This was not a temporary respite from evil. This was the ultimate victory. This was the final conquest.

But looking upon the angel, the guards found that *"his countenance was like lightning, and his raiment white as snow: and for fear of him the keepers did shake, and be-*

---

[1] Philip Schaff, quoted in *A Treasury of the Christian Faith*, S. I. Stuber and T. C. Clark, eds. (New York: Association Press, 1949), p. 92.

came as dead men." And small wonder that they did! Nobody expected this to happen. Nobody was looking for an earthquake. Nobody thought an empty tomb was possible. A Galilean carpenter had made himself obnoxious. Rome had paid as little heed to him as possible, but when he kept annoying her officials, Rome had crucified him. That, Rome thought, was that; and so in fact thought everybody else. But now it looked as if Rome had been wrong. It looked as if God was on the side of the man whom Rome had crucified; and if this was true, the world was different than they had always assumed. Loving enemies, doing good to those who hate you, turning the other cheek, walking the second mile, bearing your own cross—this was the substance of the Galilean's preaching, and if God upheld that point of view, it was not strange that guards should shake and keepers tremble. The old foundations of their self-assurance were being pulled away from their feet; they had nothing on which to stand; and they "became as dead men."

"And the angel answered and said unto the women, Fear not ye: for I know that ye seek Jesus, which was crucified. He is not here: for he is risen as he said. Come, see the place where the Lord lay!" Is there no significance in the fact that the angel's words were not addressed to the guards but to the women? The keepers had good reason for their fears: their world was crashing down around their heads. But not so with the women: their world was finding new foundations, and their world was being lighted with a fresh, new proof of permanence.

The crucified Christ was not in the tomb. "He is not here," the angel had told them. "He is not here: for he is risen as he said." And down the halls of time that confidence has lifted up the fainting hearts of men until in the days of the Second World War Margaret Slattery could write those words of haunting beauty:

> There are graves in the lonely sands of Africa where a brother who died bravely was buried; a dear beloved friend; a boy who won at tennis and swam across the lake with strong steady strokes a few short months ago. They were buried where they fell and the tide of battle roared on leaving a mound, a cross, a flag. Above such graves there is a voice saying, *He is not here*.
>
> In far-away Bataan they buried a nurse who had been good and gay and very daring; a doctor who with his last ounce of strength had ministered to those in pain; and a Filipino patriot, one of his country's finest sons. Over their graves a voice in the wind, a clear voice is saying, *Not here—not here —because I live—they live also*.

Mary Magdalene and the other Mary had come to the garden "to see the sepulchre," and that was all they ever *would* see in that rocky tomb. They could see the place where the Lord lay, but the Lord himself was no longer there. He had risen as he said, and already that sequence of events had been initiated out of which would come the Christian faith, the Christian gospel, the Christian church. It has been said that "not one line of the New Testament was written—not one sentence, whether of Gospels, Epistles, Acts or Apocalypse, was penned, apart from the conviction that He of whom these things were being written had conquered death and was alive forever." [2] And in the events of this one tremendous day that faith had taken root. Jesus Christ was not dead! He was alive!

[2] James S. Stewart, *A Faith to Proclaim* (New York: Scribner, 1953), p. 105.

But now turn back to the angel again. "Come, see the place where the Lord lay," he had said, *"and go quickly, and tell his disciples that he is risen from the dead; and, behold, he goeth before you into Galilee; there shall ye see him: lo, I have told you."* Come, see—and go, tell! The rocky tomb was not to be made a private chapel. There was to be no secret fellowship of those who, having been the witnesses of strange events, retained them for their own enjoyment only. Come, see—and go, tell! Already the faith was being turned into a gospel. The disciples must be informed. The disciples must be convinced. And as the risen Lord moved outward into endless Galilees beyond the borders of Jerusalem, the ones who loved him must go with him. The resurrection was not the final chapter in the book of God's greatest purpose: it was only the first, and although the disciples must be told at once, already preparations must also be made for something reaching far beyond them. It was in the northern fishing villages that they would find their next assignment. It was in their homes, with their friends, at their work, among the men who hated them. And so having come, they were quickly to go; and having gone, they had the promise that they would behold once more the One whom they had never thought to see again.

"And they departed quickly from the sepulchre with fear and great joy; and did run to bring his disciples word." They ran with great joy because they had been told that their Lord was still alive, but they ran with fear because they could not help but wonder if the word were really true. They ran with fear because they knew what Rome had done at Golgotha and still could do to those she hated, but they ran with great joy because if Christ had risen from the dead, it did not matter any more what Rome might do to them. But whether with fear or with great joy,

THE DAY OF THE EARTHQUAKE

they ran. That was all that really mattered. Their doubts, their uncertainties, their weaknesses, their imperfections—all these they put behind them. They did as they were told. They started to preach the gospel of the risen Lord. They ran to bring his disciples word.

"And as they went to tell his disciples, behold, Jesus met them, saying, All hail. And they came and held him by the feet, and worshipped him." It was as simple as that. They obeyed, and they found. They believed, and they were confirmed in their belief. They ran to tell, and they themselves were told.

Many years later someone would say that

"one must practice the doing of things even before one knows how to do them. . . . We have to cook before we know how to cook. We have to hammer and saw, clumsily and with grotesque results, before we can become a carpenter. We have to stumble and fall if we are to walk. The only way in which we can grow into something better than we are now is to do things we are not strictly able to do." [3]

That was what happened in the women at the tomb. They preached before they knew how to preach. They taught before they knew that they could teach. They proclaimed the faith which they had before they possessed the faith which they wished that they had. When they did, "Jesus met them," and over and over again the experience of the women has been sustained in the hearts of those who followed their example. The risen Christ did not appear to Pilate. He did not come to Caiaphas. He was not demonstrated to the multitude which had demanded that Rome should crucify him. He came to the women who had loved him. He came to the disciples who had

[3] Samuel H. Miller, *The Life of the Soul* (New York: Harper, 1951), p. 17.

followed him. He came to the people who had trusted him. And when they saw him, they "held him by the feet and worshipped him"; for now death had lost its sting, and the grave had been robbed of its victory, and peace had passed their understanding, and life had overcome the world.

After John Brown had been hanged, Thoreau remarked of him, "I meet him at every turn. He is more alive than ever he was." So, too, it is with Christ today. On highway and byway, in factor and marketplace, in home and school, and in the hearts of people one by one—there still we meet him in our crowded days. We meet him in blessing, or we meet him in judgment. But we cannot get away from him. For "lo," he said, "I am with you always, even unto the end of the world."

14

WHAT DIFFERENCE DOES EASTER MAKE?

by JAMES A. PIKE

Bishop, the Episcopal Diocese of California, San Francisco

WHY DO we have Easter? It's not simply the celebration of something long ago. It's the reaffirmation of something in the present, that can mean everything to every one of us. For many it is a sort of folk festival. We see fancier hats, new clothes; it stands for the rebirth of Spring, and so forth. But this isn't the reason Easter began. Easter came because Jesus Christ, put to death on the Cross, rose again from the dead. This made all the difference to everyone who knows it now.

Why do we believe that Jesus Christ rose from the dead? The first thing we know is that he told us that he would. And those who think of him as just a great teacher, or who say he is the greatest man that ever lived, are in a logical difficulty if they deny that he told the truth in this regard. If he did not rise from the dead, that would mean either that he was deluded, or that he was a charlatan. And if he were either of those, he was no proper leader of men, let alone the greatest man that ever lived.

But there's a further reason: if the Cross were the end for him; if he who proclaimed the victory in eternal life, proclaimed his kingdom to be invincible, were to be done in by men, it would mean the reversal of everything he taught. He taught that good was stronger than evil, that God is stronger than men, that the Kingdom of Heaven is more important than the kingdoms of this world. If the Cross were the end, it would prove that evil is stronger than goodness, that hate is stronger than love, that men are stronger than God, that the kingdoms of this world are stronger than the Kingdom of God.

And then there's another reason. The apostles were not particularly notable men, not particularly brave men. Most of them didn't show up near the end and apparently none really were at the Cross with him, though perhaps the Apostle John tarried. They were scared—they'd given up. But when they felt anew the reality of his presence among them, they were changed men, they became powerful men. They went out and preached at the risk of their lives; in fact, all but one did end as a martyr. It's hard to believe that they would have made up the story, made up their experience, because it was so disadvantageous to go around saying the things they said. The fact that they said it meant that they felt compelled by its truth, even to take the risk of telling others about it, under penalty of law.

It is more plausible to believe, then, that the Gospel story is true. It's more difficult to believe that it is not true. So I say to you, if you've had difficulty in believing this story, just consider how difficult it is not to believe the story.

Of course, the Gospel accounts themselves are somewhat ambiguous and divided as to the manner of our Lord's resurrection. St. Paul suggests that he had a psychical body: that is, not a physical body, but a means of expression and communication by which others could know his presence. The evangelists are divided as to whether it was a physical resurrection. It's not the same kind of a body that walks through a door, as one account tells us, and that eats a fish, as another account tells us. And so for Christians ever since, the question has been open about the way that God made Christ evident to the Apostles.

The way is not important. What is important is the fact

WHAT DIFFERENCE DOES EASTER MAKE?

of it: they knew that he was really in their presence. On the road to Emmaus, two of them were talking the day after all these things happened. They were discouraged, for they had hoped that Jesus might save Israel. They felt someone joining them, and they sat down at a meal, and there was the breaking of bread. The Gospel tells us, "They knew him in the breaking of bread." Then he vanished. Just what his presence was like, we don't need to know. And yet Christians all through the centuries, many in their churches today and throughout this Eastertide, know him in the breaking of bread. They've known his real presence among them, though not always knowing just how. The fact is enough for their faith, for their conviction, for their action.

In this we know then the victory of God, we know the victory of goodness, we know the victory of love. But what does that say to us? We have our crosses; we suffer many things, where evil seems triumphant; and, more than that, we come to death ourselves. What will happen to us? In the resurrection of Christ is the promise of what will happen to us.

The great words of Scripture that form the Eastertide Canticle for so many of us tie these things up together. I'll read them to you, in this case from the *Book of Common Prayer:*

"Christ, our Passover, is sacrificed for us; therefore let us keep the feast, not with the old leaven, neither with the leaven of malice and wickedness, but with the unleavened bread of sincerity and truth." And here's the key point:

"Christ being raised from the dead, dieth no more; Death hath no more dominion over Him, for in that He died, He died unto sin once, but in that He liveth, He liveth unto God. Likewise reckon ye also yourselves to be dead indeed unto sin, but alive unto God through Jesus Christ,

JAMES A. PIKE

Our Lord. Christ is risen from the dead, and become the first fruits of them that slept. For since by man came death, by man came also the resurrection of the dead; for as in Adam all die, even so in Christ shall all be made alive."

And by *all,* that means all of you, it means me; we shall be made alive, and death will not be the end of us.

What will life be like ahead? I have no blueprint for that. The particular tradition in Christendom in which I stand happens to think we cannot blueprint it very well. But we can know certain things: that the God who gave us life intended us to keep that life forever; that the God who gave us individuality, particularity, peculiarity, intends us to remain individual, particular, and peculiar forever.

The Bible and the Christian creeds do not talk much about immortality of the soul, as though the soul itself sort of automatically joins other spiritual bodies and is absorbed in some kind of oblong blur, some kind of oversoul. There are reasons to believe in the immortality of the soul for philosophical reasons. But what we proclaim is the resurrection of the body. "I believe in . . . . the resurrection of the body"—that's what the Creed says. Not this body, of course. Everything that is now my body will be dead in seven years.

What does body mean? Some of you in your homes are understanding something of my thoughts and catching something of my spirit today. But you are not in touch with my thoughts nor my spirit; you're in touch with a television receiver. And that machine can pick up what the camera men have picked up—all physical things. And what are they picking up? They're picking up a physical body. They're picturing movements of a hand. They're seeing muscular changes in a face. They're recording a very physical voice, which is coming into very physical microphones and reaching you through a very physical receiver. It's only through my body that you can know me at all. It's only through a body that we can communicate one with another, can relate ourselves one to another, can remain individuals, different and distinct one from another.

And so it is, our faith and the Bible tell us, in the life to come. We will be provided with a means of communication, of relationship, and of separation one from another, that we may better join each other in the relationship of one personality to another; that we may understand each other and enjoy each other.

So we proclaim the resurrection of the body as a gift of God, and not as an inherent right of the soul. Now from a philosophical point of view, it can be argued that immortality of the soul is more plausible than not; and I think it's worth tarrying on that for a moment. My spirit now transcends my body. When I'm asleep, my mind's at work. I thought last night as I was going to sleep about what I was going to say to you today, and when I woke up this morning, a lot of it was really worked out. My mind had been working while my body wasn't active.

More than that, we are more than ourselves. We can change ourselves; we can, for example, through diet even change the shape of ourselves. We are over and above ourselves. More than that, all the principal hungers of life have a real fulfillment to meet them. People hunger for food. Well, sometimes they may not find enough food in one place or another in the world—but there *is* food—there is something to match that hunger. People hunger for sexual fulfillment. Again, not everyone has things worked out as to that aspect of his life; but there is such a thing as a fulfillment for that particular hunger. And so it goes, right through all the principal hungers of man.

Now man has always hungered for eternal life. He doesn't feel this life is enough; he knows things aren't complete; he knows that wrongs are not righted; he knows that friendships are not completed; he knows that things have not been accomplished that belong to the fulfillment of his own personality. And it's reasonable to believe that matching every other hunger of man there is a fulfillment. And it's reasonable to believe in immortality of the soul . . .

But what the Gospel proclaims is the resurrection of the body, not resting on any of our arguments, but upon the fact that God gives us this gift and has proven it, because Jesus Christ was made known as risen from the dead.

This is what created the Christian church. This was the method. This was the whole reason for the new Israel in the fulfillment and carrying out of the old Israel, the covenant which began with Abraham. This is the reason Sunday began. They wanted to celebrate this great event right away, and so they chose the first day of the week, the day on which Jesus rose.

What will we be like in the life to come? Well, again I would admit that this particular body is not going to survive, but I would affirm that God will supply us a way of communication, of relationship. St. Paul suggests this in the beautiful passage which is used in so many burial services. He raises the question: "Some men will say, how are the dead raised up, and with what body do they come?" And then he turns to the analogy of the seed in the ground and the flower of the plant. "That which thou sowest is not quickened, except it die. That which thou sowest, thou sowest not that body that shall be, but bare grain, it may chance of wheat, or some other grain. But God giveth it a body as it hath pleased him." And he goes on to say that every type of animal has a different kind of body suitable to its purposes and different stars have different magnitudes. God in his greatness and versatility can find the way in the life to come for us *to be ourselves*.

WHAT DIFFERENCE DOES EASTER MAKE?

Now, one naturally asks the question: "Will we know each other there?" And the answer is, Yes! Because we believe firmly that in the life to come I will not be less myself, I will be more myself. I will more and more become my full self, which in this life I have not fully become. And every one of you will be more yourself than you are now.

And, of course, since love is eternal and since individuality is eternal, and since we are what we are so much because of relations with other people, we can assume, as indeed we have been promised, that we shall be known and we shall know. In fact, this is part of what we'll be busy with—getting to know each other better and better. So little time in this world is given us to know enough people well. And how exciting any individual person is, no matter how dull they may have seemed in the beginning—if you really get to know them, if you really *try* to know them, if you're open to them. What a variety of people there are! And how exciting the life to come will be when you consider that people of all ages, all centuries will be there, and that we'll all get to know each other. There are so many people that *I* want to know. I'm sure you'd have your own list also. So there's an infinite variety of possibilities. And there is an eternity of time.

And one might ask, "What about heaven and hell?" Maybe we won't get to talk to each other, because we'll be in different places. Well, it's hard to say it, but there's simply got to be a hell and here's why. It's not that I have any particular people in mind I'd like to be there. It's not just to work off my own aggressions that I say that. But the reason for hell is *human freedom*. God took the great risk of allowing all of us to be free, which means the risk to be free to be against him. We are free to shake our fists at God—we are free to shake our fists at him through all eternity, if we insist upon doing so. And God will not cramp our freedom. He will seek to lure us toward him. He will seek to attract us. He will surround us with others who will seek to move us toward him and turn us toward him; but he will not force us. He believes in freedom that much.

In other words, he won't make us go to heaven if we don't *want* to. And what is hell? It's very simple. Hell is separation from God. It means "missing the boat". It means having missed the important thing: being right with the ultimate ground of all creation—the One who made you, the One who calls you, the One who you have been made to adore and serve. What is heaven? Heaven is being right with God. It means that there's no barrier of separation between you and him.

Oddly enough, we can experience these things right now. You don't need to wait till death to know something of each. If God used all the imagination he's capable of—and I'm sure that he will—to produce the most glorious possible kind of heaven, if he really fulfilled all the lovely things in the quaint old hymns that are sometimes naive in describing the details of heaven, if he did all this and more, still he could confer upon us nothing greater than being right with him. And that we can have right now. So heaven has nothing greater to offer than what you can have right now: being right with God— forgiven by his grace, accepted by him, being part of his cause in the world.

On the other hand, if God were a kind of Jonathan Edwards God, who spent his time thinking up the worst tortures and rejoiced in dangling the souls over the eternal fire to see them seared and singed—even if he were that way, he could think up nothing worse than being separated from him. And this we can have right now. Being separated from him is the worst thing that can be thought

WHAT DIFFERENCE DOES EASTER MAKE?

up, and we can be that way *now* if we wish. It's all a question of the use of our freedom.

What if we die and we were separated from God? What happens? Or what if we die and we're essentially on God's side, but not perfect? There have been certain pockets of resistance—certain hatreds, certain prejudices. What about that in the life to come? Well, here especially I think it's well to realize we don't know too much. We can't affirm answers to questions like that with the same certainty as we can affirm the *fact* of eternal life— and the *fact* of redemption through Christ.

But I think we can infer a good deal from the nature of God as we know him now. He never lets us down. He always seeks us. He always follows up. He's like a man rowing all the way around an island, trying to find a place to land. He wants to get us to turn. I can't believe that his nature changes—and turning to the human side of the matter, I don't think there's any man on earth that's been so bad, so turned away from God and his fellow man, that there aren't some dying embers there that God can fan into flame. And God wants that soul. He wants that man on his side.

On the other hand, I don't think any man's ever died— I don't care if he has "Saint" in front of his name or not— who was so perfect in every human relationship, every human response, from the days of his cradle all the way to his death, that there are not a few things needing ironing out, a few places where he's got to give up some prejudice, some hatred, some resentment, some misconception, and yield it up to God and become God's man totally. Therefore, it's reasonable to think that after we die, things'll be much as they are with us, except we're in a greater light, we're in closest fellowship of the communion of those who have gone on beyond, and will be seeking to cause us to turn, to give up this, to give up that, to seek this better objective, to respond to someone we never responded to before, to be open to people of races we've perhaps never been very friendly with before.

I'm sure that this process is enough to keep everybody there busy, working on each other, because it's a process in freedom—it's experience in free change in response to God's action. And it may be—there have been those all through the centuries who have so hoped at least—that the time may come when *all* will have turned, when God will be all in all. There will be no pockets of resistance, and this is really his victory and the victory of his kingdom.

You found on this earth that it's not a victory over someone when you stamp them out or when you push them off from you. That's not a victory. It's a victory when you've won them—when you've made friends, and you've removed a barrier. And God's greatest victory will be not that some are against him—but that all, finally, are for him. One can hope that.

That's why we should pray for those who have gone on beyond, just as we pray for those who are with us now, holding them before God in our concern. And we can assume that those who have gone on beyond are praying for us as a kind of heavenly rooting section as we run our earthly race.

Meanwhile, we now can settle this question of heaven or hell. We can decide freely to be on God's side—to give up those things which separate us from him, to accept his forgiving grace, and in a sense, die to other allegiances as final allegiances. If we die now we won't have to fear the second death. If we die now, we have already entered eternal life, we have that which is essential to heaven. God will even now be our one and only central Ruler and

WHAT DIFFERENCE DOES EASTER MAKE?

Guide of our being. We will not be separated from him, but be united with him in his purposes. This is the time to do it.

One might say, "Well, if you can work it out later, what's the hurry now?" The trouble is, the longer you wait, the longer you are missing heaven now. And, second, I've told you that I *speculate* that you'll be able to work it out later. But this isn't something as firm as all that, because other Christians think otherwise. I think it kinder to your others who've died to follow the position I've taken, and to assume that they'll make the grade someday, and hence to pray for them, and hope for them—even if you weren't so sure about them when they were living on this earth. But as to yourself, I think you'd better take that more strict view that maybe death settles it. I don't think it does—but it's safer to play it that way, I think. I wouldn't like any of you to arrive at the pearly gates and be barred, and try to explain to St. Peter that that Dr. Pike told you one Eastertide that you'd have another chance. He might say, "We never heard of him here."

So it's better to make your decision now. "Now is the time of salvation," our Lord said. And another word from him: "Walk in the light while ye have the light ere the darkness cometh." We can so protect ourselves with defence-mechanisms and excuses as to hide ourselves both from criticism of others and from our own self-criticism that maybe we won't hear the knocking of God. Maybe we will have made the walls too thick. And it's just possible that though God will always knock, even deep into eternity, the time might come that we can't hear anymore. And so for yourself and your decisions now, don't count on what I've said. Yet one can hope that all will finally be saved, because God would want it that way.

There's an old prayer that I think it might be well to

say as we tie our present life into the life to come, as we count on the resurrection of Christ as bringing us new life to come. I'll read it to you:

"O God, whose days are without end, and whose mercies cannot be numbered; Make us, we beseech Thee, deeply sensible of the shortness and uncertainty of human life; And let Thy Holy Spirit lead us in holiness and righteousness, all our days: that when we shall have served Thee in our generation, we may be gathered unto our fathers, having the testimony of a good conscience; in the Communion of the catholic Church; in the confidence of a certain faith; in the comfort of a reasonable, religious, and holy hope, in favor with Thee our God, and in perfect charity with the world. All of which we ask, through Jesus Christ, our Lord."

This Eastertide, meditate upon these things. Know that Christ is risen from the dead—that Christ has fulfilled the hopes of his people, that they could not put him out of the world by death, that he is with us, and that his eternal life made manifest plainly to his followers, has been made manifest throughout the centuries in the breaking of the bread, and is made manifest in the Christian fellowship throughout the centuries. Here we have the ground of our eternal hope.

If the philosophical speculations about immortality appeal to you, as they do to me—fine. That will encourage you. But you have something more than speculation. You have the affirmation, you have the *fact* that Christ rose from the dead. The fact is the reason for all that's happened in the world since in terms of Christian belief, Christian ethics, and Christian culture. And in that is *your* hope for eternal life—as well as for life, true life, now.

THE UNSEEN EASTER

by LISTON POPE

Dean, Divinity School of Yale University,
New Haven, Connecticut

AN INTELLIGENT and successful friend of mine told me recently that he is appalled by the notion that he might live forever. He said, "I am sick of myself, even before I am old, and the idea that I might go on being myself forever is too dreadful to contemplate."

There is no way of knowing whether he spoke from modesty or shame or world-weariness. Nor can one know whether his attitude is widely shared by other people. Certainly the desire for personal immortality has been renounced by many thoughtful persons. George Bernard Shaw once designated as the ultimate in selfishness the hope that one's own puny life would go on forever. The German poet Heine cried out:

To vegetate through all eternity . . .

. . . no such everlastingness for me.

God, if he can, keep me from such a plight.

Repudiation of immortality was voiced as pungently, if less elegantly, by the man who instructed that on his tombstone should be inscribed:

Don't bother me now,

Don't bother me never.

I want to be dead

Forever and ever.

If similar attitudes are widespread, the Easter faith by so much is dead, and the celebration of Easter is only a spring festival. The visible celebration encircles the earth today. Thousands rose to greet the sunrise this morning in Palestine, where once an empty tomb was found. It is Easter on Fifth Avenue, with its annual story of fashions on parade. It is Easter in great cathedrals where candles burn on high altars, and in bare chapels in Africa, and on ships at sea and caravans in the desert. In every continent, the celebration of Easter can be seen. Everywhere, everywhere, Easter today.

But what is that to us, unless it is Easter in our hearts? What matters it how gay Fifth Avenue may be if one's own soul is lifeless and deserted and if life is viewed as only a dead-end street leading to the grave? More important than all the pomp and pageantry that greet the eye is the unseen celebration of the Easter faith deep in our own spirits. For what is the world's Easter but a passing show unless in our own souls we have intimations that life is more than that?

Doubtless many of us do reach out quietly but eagerly on this day in search of the faith that Christ has triumphed over death. There are those who have lost, since Easter last was here, many whom they had loved, and perhaps even their very dearest one, and their thoughts turn today toward the mystery beyond the shadow. There are those on whom the dust of life has settled, who are tired in body and spirit, who question whether St. Paul spoke truly in saying that the inward man is renewed day by day. There are all of us, living a few years on a planetary speck whirling in an unmeasured universe, and we peer out over the rim of the world with a surmise or a question. Are there any eternal, imperishable, everlasting things, surviving the destruction of time and death? Was St. Paul correct in saying, "The things which are seen are temporal; but the things which are not seen are eternal."

THE UNSEEN EASTER

Assuredly the things which are seen are temporal and transitory. So far as the eye will be able to perceive, Easter will have gone by tomorrow, leaving only litter. The finest gown on the avenue will fall to shreds at last and the jauntiest promenader will again be dust. "Change and decay in all around we see." The things which are seen are temporal.

In contrast to the easy denunciation of material and temporal things, we need to remember that they have a proper place. On this earth spirit must be incarnated in body; the candle of life must burn from some candlestick. Jesus Christ himself became incarnate in human flesh, and he had pity on the physical needs of the hungry, the halt, the blind. Though every house must fall and every church spire topple at last, such buildings may serve for a time as habitations for the spirit of man. Smiles and sparkling eyes, a gentle touch, echoing laughter and a remembered voice and the sound of pattering feet—these too are temporal things destined to be lost in the unreturning years. But it is right that we hold them dear. The things which are seen are temporal, but they are often lovely and of good report.

We need hardly be reminded of the importance of temporal things, of the things which are seen. Doubtless most of us live more largely by vision than by faith. Seeing is believing, and we doubt the reality of the unseen. Our civilization exalts physical, tangible values to the highest place and questions the value of that which cannot be shown to be immediately useful.

We may contrast this outlook with the civilization of Florence during the Renaissance. When the artist Giotto completed a picture there near the beginning of the fourteenth century, the entire town escorted it from the artist's studio to St. Mark's Cathedral, where it was to be hung, singing and scattering flowers as they went. Our own civilization is incomparably more productive of bathtubs, automobiles, refrigerators, and television sets than of beauty or the intangible values of the spirit. For all of our wealth and our one hundred and seventy million inhabitants, we have yet to match that one Italian town in matters of the spirit and in production of Dante, Andrea del Sarto, Michelangelo, Leonardo da Vinci, Savonarola, Giotto, and many another man of genius. We shall not do so until we can produce people like those who escorted Giotto's painting.

We desperately need to learn that the unseen things of life are the fundamental, enduring, eternal things. Nobody has ever seen faith, hope, courage, love. We have seen but faint reflections of them. Yet these are the qualities that animate our bodies and mould other physical things to their purposes. These are the powers, along with the unseen magic of the human mind, that build homes and skyscrapers and churches, that really underlie our material civilization. These are the qualities that make us what we truly are, as distinguished from what other people see.

These unseen things comprise the essence of the human soul. They are eternal. There is no visible, scientific evidence that this is so. The philosopher William James examined all the evidence and arguments for and against immortality, and concluded that science and reason can neither prove nor disprove its truth. There are many mysteries here that will never be solved by human ingenuity.

But evidence for the life everlasting can be found in the deepest experiences and intuitions of the soul. Life can be lived here and now to significant degree in an unseen, invisible realm, and experiences in that realm can bring their own conviction that death does not reign supreme. The New Testament reminds us that "no man hath seen

THE UNSEEN EASTER

God at any time." But, as was said of Moses, we can endure here and now as seeing him who is invisible. "Now, ... now ... abideth faith, hope, love." Eternity begins now; heaven reflects its rays on the earth.

Beyond the reach of all science and all reason lies this faith. It has seldom been expressed more clearly than by Victor Hugo at the age of seventy:

"I feel in myself the future life. . . . I am rising, I know, toward the sky . . . You say the soul is nothing but the resultant of the bodily powers. Why, then, is my soul more luminous when my bodily powers begin to fail? Winter is on my head, but eternal spring is in my heart. . . . The tomb is not a blind alley; it is a thoroughfare. It closes on the twilight, opens on the dawn."

Beyond all the intimations of the human spirit, faith in Christ the risen Lord opens vistas of immortality. The central meaning of his resurrection is not that of providing immortality for you and me; Christ rose again that God should not be mocked by the power of Satan and death. He rose again that you and I might believe and be endowed on their earth with the power of his Spirit. Because he lives, we too shall live.

Is it not the most amazing story man has ever heard? Once long ago the door of a tomb was closed with a huge stone, and a military guard was placed outside, lest one whose broken body had been put there should rise as he had promised. Surely this was the end of his story. Those who had watched him die and had placed him in the tomb were utterly bereft. His disciples scattered in hopelessness. All the promises he had made seemed now illusions; all the faith they had reposed in him seemed now mislaid. But the story was not finished. It goes on to say that an angel of the Lord, symbolic of God's infinite power and unshakable purpose, descended from heaven and rolled the stone away, and proclaimed a risen Christ. Their Master returned to the disciples and became a living presence beyond the tomb. They found it difficult to believe. Thomas refused to believe until he had seen the print of the nails and felt the rent in the side. Jesus rebuked him by saying: "Have you believed because you have seen me? Blessed are those who have not seen and yet believed."

For twenty centuries Christ's followers have believed though they have not seen. And many have reported that they have known his living presence in their own lives. For in the unseen realm of the spirit he is always reliving his life. In every age, Christ lives and works and dies and rises. He is born again and again. In our lives, shabby stables though they are, he may be cradled. He grows again, and those in whom he grows come to wisdom and stature. He comes again to our temples and confounds the learned and the wise. He comes with healing and forgiveness; the blind see, and the lame walk, and we being evil know how to give good gifts. He comes with imperious demands, so that we are never easy in our comfort, never adequate in our love. He will not let us be, this ruler of eternity who struggles with the souls of every age.

And how often he dies—not once at Calvary, but on a thousand battle-scarred hills and in a thousand hearts that take their ease. Always he rises again to keep his pledge that he will be with us always, even unto the end. This morning he is there in the churches and cathedrals, and there in the bitter slums, and there in your own life. In the darkest times he comes very near.

Always he stands at the door of the soul, and knocks. And whenever he enters that unseen realm, the Easter story comes alive again, and there is an inner resurrection that brooks no denying, and we are lifted above our former selves.

THE UNSEEN EASTER

Perhaps most of us do not wish to live forever if we must continue to live as we are. Creatures of body and sense, we know the ills that flesh is heir to. Creatures of spirit, we know how pride and fear can warp even our souls. Our lives become shabby vehicles of pain and fear. But if any man is in Christ Jesus, he is a new creature. And in his new estate he has a foretaste of the glory of the life everlasting.

Let us then keep an unseen Easter in our hearts—not in order that a conventional holiday be celebrated there, but in response to the entreaties of Christ himself, who rose again and rises still. Only then shall we know that the things which are unseen are eternal and that truly Christ rose from the dead.

Breathe on us, Breath of God,
So shall we never die,
But live with thee the perfect life
Of thine eternity.

16

THE GLADNESS OF GOD

by DAVID H. C. READ

Pastor, Madison Avenue Presbyterian Church,
New York, New York

"Then were the disciples glad, when they saw the Lord."

—JOHN 20:20

EASTER is here, and the Christian church pulls out all the stops. The muted praise of Lent and Holy Week is now released in a crescendo of joy and adoration from crowded congregations across the Christian world. Ancient cathedrals tremble with the resurrection music and their windows glow anew in the Easter light as the Christian past joins with the present to hold high festival. Little country churches, aflame with daffodils and lilies take up the song, and in our modern cities every device in our electronic world is pressed into service, and every wire, every wave, is alive with alleluias. From the worshiping crowds the Easter song rises in a tide that overflows the walls of our churches and cascades across the waiting world, rousing echoes of hope and joy—the age-long yearning of the human heart for life renewed.

What words can the Christian preacher find to set in the midst of the Easter music? Though he speak with the tongue of men and of angels he cannot compete with the sounding brass. In preparation he paces his study. The volumes of theology gather round him and offer the

THE GLADNESS OF GOD

weighty words of the greatest Christian thinkers about the significance of the resurrection. He lets them talk, then reaches for the poets. Words he must find, if not the polysyllabic explications of the theologians, then the winged and soaring loveliness of metaphor and image, the magic word that explodes in the mind like a star in a velvet night. Somewhere there must be radiant rhetoric in which to clothe this message of Easter joy. Somewhere—yes, and where else but in the records of the first Easter Day? And so to the Gospels, and what does he find? No music, no trumpets, no alleluias, no rhetoric, no theological argument, no poetry. Just a few words about an empty tomb, a scrap of conversation about a gardener, a simple statement that the crucified Jesus appeared to a few men and women—and the whole thing summed up in the words, "Then were the disciples glad, when they saw the Lord."

That's how the Bible speaks. Ten words, and all except one are monosyllables. A child could understand. And, just because it is so simple, an adult could fail to understand. For beneath the theology of two thousand years, behind the swelling adoration of the universal church, basic to the entire fabric of our Easter celebration, is this single fact—that a few ordinary men and women saw Jesus alive again and were glad.

Simple words can often cover the very deepest emotion. In fact the things that move us most need no elaboration. Plain words will do. At a meeting the other day I was recalling what it felt like to be suddenly released after five years as a prisoner-of-war. I remember, as if it were yesterday, the moment of liberation and the first free allied soldier that I saw. He was an American colonel I met at the Stalag gate. He was looking rather confused as 10,000 prisoners were surging out of the barracks in dazed excitement. I held out my hand and said: "Sir, I'm glad to see you—and that's an understatement."

An understatement. When St. John's Gospel tells us just this—that Jesus the Liberator, the conqueror of sin and death, appeared and the disciples were glad to see him—this is surely the greatest understatement of all time. And yet it conveys to us, as no flourish of rhetoric or roll of verbal drums could possibly do, the Easter fact on which our faith must rest. And as we think of what these short words imply we may come to an understanding that could make this Easter alive for us with a new power, or even become a turning-point in our lives.

What we have to do this Easter morning is to discover, or re-discover, what made the disciples glad. There wouldn't be too many people glad in Jerusalem that day. I imagine that Pilate, the Roman governor, was not too happy about the report he would have to make to Rome, and the chances are that his wife was still tormented with bad dreams. Herod and his party had probably spent the night carousing and while conscience might not trouble him a good hangover most certainly would. In the homes of the members of the Sanhedrin conscience would surely be at work, and among the ordinary people of Jerusalem that first Easter would be dismal enough, the Passover Festival ended and the streets filled with tired, departing pilgrims, irritable parents and wailing children—and unhappy memories. Perhaps it was a wet day. (Why do we always assume that the sun shone brilliantly on that first Easter?) And for most of the time the disciples of Jesus were the most miserable of all. The Messiah was dead: and not one of them had lifted a finger to save him—except Peter who had slashed out with his sword in the Garden of Gethsemane, and then a few hours later had

THE GLADNESS OF GOD

utterly denied his Lord. You can hardly picture a more dejected, disillusioned, miserable group of men and women than those who would now be called the *former* disciples of Jesus.

And then "they were glad." If I were to ask you why, you would say that the answer is obvious and that you have heard it Easter after Easter in the church. They were glad because the one they believed dead had shown himself alive again. They were glad because their dearest friend had returned from the grave. We all have some kind of a picture like this in the back of our minds—miserable disciples suddenly rejoicing as the Easter dawn reveals to them their Risen Lord.

But is this true? Is it even probable? Let me ask you this: if you lost a very dear friend in sudden death, and then after two days you suddenly saw him materialize in front of you, exactly as he was—would you immediately and spontaneously be overcome with joy and delight? Would you really be glad? I believe that you and I would be frankly terrified. We should most likely ring for the nearest psychiatrist.

If you read the accounts of what happened on Easter morning you will find something very similar. It may surprise you to find nothing about joy and gladness among the disciples at the tomb and on their way home. Our text belongs to Easter evening, not morning. The first reaction of the disciples was fear and incredulity. In the records I find the words "perplexed," "afraid," "amazed," "affrighted," "idle tales"—but not joy or gladness. In fact in St. Mark's Gospel the original manuscript comes to an end with the words "for they were afraid." It is this kind of honest reporting that has led many a skeptic to believe the resurrection story. If the church had invented it, wouldn't the authors have made the joybells ring and given us a Hallelujah Chorus by the empty tomb? But this is factual reporting. The disciples, faced with a sudden return of their Master from the dead, were scared. They thought they had seen a ghost.

How then, later in the day, did they come to be glad? This is the real Easter question for us and with its answer we touch the inner secret of the gospel. Too often and too easily we have supposed that our Easter joy rests on the fact that a man who was dead came alive again. That, in itself, is no occasion for joy—especially as we are told that the appearances only lasted for a few days.

What happened to the disciples during that first Easter Day, what happened to the infant church as they thought over this event, was something quite different from this. "Then were the disciples glad, when they saw the Lord." What mattered was not that someone had returned from the dead, but that the *Lord* had risen. This wasn't a psychic manifestation: it was a unique action of God. This was no ghost who appeared among them, "the doors being shut": it was *Jesus,* the Lord of love who had been crucified, the unique Son of God in whom alone they had seen reflected the glory of the Father. The one who had been crushed to death beneath the sins and sorrows of the world was alive again. "Then . . . came Jesus and stood in the midst and saith unto them, Peace be unto you. And when he had so said, he shewed unto them his hands and his side." "Then"—when at last it dawned on them that the Christ of God, the same Christ whose hands had been pierced with the nails and whose side was wounded with the spear, was alive—"then were the disciples glad."

Do you see what made them glad? It was not just that their friend had come back. *It was the knowledge that*

THE GLADNESS OF GOD

God had raised his crucified Son from the dead. When he stood before them still bearing the marks of the nails, saying, "Peace be unto you," the nervous fear and shock vanished from their hearts. This was Jesus the victim of the sins and wickedness of men—and now he stood before them the victor over all the powers of darkness. He stood before them as living proof that the worst man can do, the uttermost a man can suffer, the massed forces of sin, and pain, and death, the concentration of demonic power, have been totally defeated. Calvary is past. It is finished. Nothing so terrible can ever happen again. This they understood as he stood before them. The Prince of Love had overcome the sharpness of death and opened the kingdom of heaven to all believers. "Then were the disciples glad, when they saw the Lord."

During the weeks of Lent we have thought much in this church about the mystery of God, the unyielding love of Christ on his way to the Cross, and the claim he makes on us as Saviour and as Lord. This morning he asks us if we know his joy. For this is his final word. Easter means that our God is a happy God. How can he be happy, we ask, as he watches our world? How can he be happy when he sees the ghastly things that happen—the agonies, the injustices, the misery, the brutality, the million futile pains? He knows. The wounds are there, the imprint of our pain in the heart of love. But in the depths of God's being there burns a sheer eternal joy. Would you have it otherwise? Would you rather that he were so enmeshed in the web of our sins and sorrows that we could never know where victory lay, and never know whether in the end of the day joy or sorrow, light or darkness, would triumph?

This was the certainty that broke upon the disciples when they saw the Lord. They saw the victor, and in his risen body shone the goodness and the gladness of God. That's why they could go out from the room and shout across the centuries: "Christ is risen;" "sin shall not have dominion over you;" "death is swallowed up in victory."

It began in that little room in Jerusalem. "When the doors were shut . . . for fear . . . came Jesus and stood in the midst." This is what he still can do. I don't know what kind of doors of fear are shut in your heart this morning. But I know of one who can come right through and say: Peace be unto you. It's not a magic trick that happens on special occasions when the sun is shining and everyone feels happy. It's a contact that we make week by week when we worship the risen Christ together and day by day as we remain in touch with him.

Let me ask you who have sought to be his followers throughout the years: Do you know anywhere else where true joy is to be found, the gladness that does not depend on transitory events? And let me ask you who are perhaps still wondering if the Christian church has anything you need, if Christ is still relevant to your life. Are you in touch with a gladness that can see you through the dark days as well as the bright, the failures as well as the successes? That's something different from surface cheerfulness—and sooner or later we need it.

Today we are not celebrating a strange event of long ago. We are in the presence of one who is alive and will respond to the least flicker of our faith and love. Christ is here. Are you glad to see him? He awaits your welcome, for he can take you, like the disciples on that first Easter, and lift you from your fears and sins into the abiding goodness and gladness of God.

17

GOD'S GREAT NEVERTHELESS

by PAUL E. SCHERER

Professor, Union Theological Seminary,
New York, New York

*"What shall we then say to these things? . . .
It is Christ that died, yea rather, that is risen
again . . ."*

—ROMANS 8:31, 34 (in part)

THAT certainly ought to settle it. You should know what to say now, how to answer back when things pile up. If you ask Paul what things, he will throw in all there is about life that's ugly and threatening: tribulation and distress, persecution and famine, nakedness, peril and sword—everything that stands up in this world of ours to contradict our being here. Then, planting his feet there squarely, he will point you to God's great "Nevertheless" —the "Christ that died" and was "risen again": that infinite rebuttal, no matter what!

The resurrection of Jesus Christ wasn't the promise of a victory some day; it was victory now. It wasn't a fact for historians, though I can find no hint anywhere that it was anything less! It was more, not less: it was a fact for people who wanted to keep on their feet when everything seemed bent on going to pieces. It was the one solid purchase a man had in the cosmic weather: and it was his the minute he was ready to quit playing with it as if it had to be weighed, maybe so, maybe not, and began instead actually to move out on it in the presence and power of the living Christ. One of the most widely known and read New Testament scholars of our time says that if the resurrection doesn't mean this it can scarcely be said to mean anything: that the strain it puts on the understanding is simply not comparable to the strain it puts on our too often complacent, but even more often anxious and defeated lives.

Let's see then, first of all, if we can spell out for ourselves the contradictions which this Easter gospel, with such a magnificent sweep, so vastly—contradicts! Perhaps we need to get one thing settled right away: it isn't a panacea for anything. It doesn't concern itself, except incidently, with the difficulties we get into: not with anybody's private peace of mind therefore; not with Western civilization and our desperate efforts to save it, notably among other things by packing all our bags and getting back as promptly as possible to religion—it is never quite clear what religion! What should be clear by this time is that "on our way back" the gods we fashion in our image, the God who fashioned us will utterly destroy! These problems of living, which send us scurrying every now and then, hysterically looking for some kind of remedy, Jesus always treated with a high hand; he bluntly dismissed most of them: not because he was lacking in compassion—he was crucified for having too much—but because getting through was what mattered to him, and not the getting out which seems to mean so much to us! Besides, he knew that getting through difficulty was almost always easier than getting through success! I wish we could remember that. It's why all the bad men in Jesus' parables were successful men. Not one of them went bankrupt, or lost his wife, or forfeited the respect of the community. Nothing happened in this world to any of them that ought to have happened!

GOD'S GREAT NEVERTHELESS

Dives was in fine fettle when he brushed by the beggar at his gate without seeing anything at all. The unjust steward got away with his plan to win friends and influence people by a little sharp practice. Your barns were filled with wheat that night when God whispered, "You fool!"

We may say then, may we not, that whatever else the gospel of the risen Lord sets out to do, it doesn't offer to make the pains of living milder, or to provide "a hedge against the brutal realities of man's brief existence"—disappointment, loneliness, frustration. Paul of all men else had reason to know that. He wasn't let off cheaply. God didn't give his Son for any such thing. If we want the true measure of this divine "Nevertheless," we dare not misread the odds. The New Testament doesn't address itself primarily to the problems of living. It addresses itself first and foremost to the problem of life! That's what we are up against; and from that there is no escape.

Ordinarily we think of life as the one precious thing we have in common; and indeed it is: the love and honor and decency and high devotion which are a light in the window and a fire on the hearth in your home and mine; the reckless beauty out there today along the roads and on the hills. God has done so well with it—if we'd only leave it alone, and not get our finger marks all over it. But to see no more than that! Like men singing some old nostalgic college song at their fiftieth reunion: says Amos Wilder, "Every eye is wet, and nobody believes a word of it!" At the end of the Spanish novel *Blood and Sand,* a matador is carried out of the ring to die, in his ears, as the book ends, the "roar of the only beast there is—humanity". Listen to it in the day's news. That has to be reckoned with too: hate, and greed, and pride, and power—the shuffling feet of homeless millions, here in this "limitless void of nature," back there the thousands of years that are gone, yonder the thousands that are yet to come, as your life and mine touch that swift stream like the brush of a swallow's wing, out of the unknown at birth, into the unknown at death, with nothing between but the inscrutable world, open at both ends, the wind blowing through it!

Then one afternoon at a party, maybe in the dusk of a summer's evening, at night when you go to bed, that world closes in on you—like the room in Edgar Allan Poe's *The Pit and the Pendulum,* with the abyss at the center, and the walls that keep crowding you toward it. "What shall we say then to these things?" "What things?" you ask, and as Paul tries to answer, "tribulation, distress," you have the growing sense of some profound contradiction to all our hopes and plans, "persecution, famine," something in the very nature of our being here, "nakedness, peril, sword," which threatens at any moment to cancel all that we are and have! I am told that the only inborn fear is the fear of falling, of having all the supports knocked out from under us. That's exactly how it feels when all at once we realize what it means to be alive! Kafka calls it the ceaseless knocking at the castle gate. You hear it in Macbeth: something trying to get into my world, maybe death; something I don't want to face, waiting out there, and I say this and that to cover it up, but I know there's no security against it. Thurneysen writes somewhere of the unknown that has me surrounded—and I catch my breath, and suddenly my throat tightens! They call that nowadays "the anxiety of existence." There is little use in giving it a name: it will be there long after the name has worn off! This it is which the New Testament addresses: not the problems of living, but the problem of life. Nothing less.

And this that's more—for mind you, you haven't solved the problem of life when you pronounce God's name: you've really succeeded only in stating it! As the Bible well

GOD'S GREAT NEVERTHELESS

knows, God himself is the problem of life! And for him there is no solution! I hear you: you want to tell me it makes no sense to say that. But let me put it to you. When you actually find out who it is that's going to be there, no matter where you turn, does it seem to you like coming home to some dear shelter, or does it seem like setting foot on the shores of an undiscovered land, never tamed, perilous and wild? Be careful with your answer. Do you not know even yet that way down in our hearts we are all set to run from the God we have to the God we want? And they talk to us about faith as if it were nothing but a defense! How can that be, when it lays you wide open! "Take heed," says the Old Testament, "take diligent heed." "Take heed," echoes the New, "let every man take heed." Paul writes of the perils he has faced, robbers, countrymen, heathen, in the city, in the wilderness, in the sea: but always as if with hushed breath he would speak of a greater —"lest that by any means, when I have preached to others, I myself should be a castaway!" Could it be that this human life of ours stands in peril of God?

Listen to the psalmist scrabbling off up hill and down dale as fast as ever his legs can carry him: "Whither shall I go from thy spirit? or whither shall I flee from thy presence?" You suppose he didn't try? "If I ascend up into heaven, thou art there,"—in the darkness as in the light, on the wings of the morning and in the uttermost parts of the earth. Who wants to be beset like that, behind and before, with such a hand on his shoulder? Nietzsche said that this was the God men had to kill, because he knows too much, and we are too ugly! At least Nietzsche understood what it was he was rebelling against! We want to identify God with what we call the good; and we are altogether in favor of the good! But what if his good should contradict ours? We say he's the true and the beautiful, and set all our little images up in his place to run our errands for us and keep us safe because we'd rather have anything but the God we have, who searches us and knows us, knows our downsitting and our uprising, understands our thought afar off. Read the Bible! Is he so lovely and congenial, asks Jaroslav Pelikan, in his *Fools for Christ*—so "warm like a rose, with all the colors of the sunset in it?" What about the day when he left Jesus on the Cross, and Stephen among the stones? What's so tender about him that he could look on men and women and children in the arena, with leopards leaping at them, and do nothing? We decorate him. The God of the Bible is naked God! We cannot prove that we love him by the tricks we play to be quit of him!

That plunges us in, I think, as far as we've got to come; but we do have to come that far, whether we like it or not, before we can even hear this Easter gospel. Now let Paul state his fact and put his question: "It is Christ that died, yea rather, that is risen again." "What shall we then say to these things?" You should know what to say now, how to answer back! "Who shall separate us from the love of Christ?" And with that he throws all common sense everywhere into reverse with a vengeance—all death and life, all height and depth, things present and things to come!

It's exactly what Jesus himself was always doing. One day he turned around and announced, "Lazarus is dead." Why on earth that wasn't the end of that, you tell me; but it wasn't! "Nevertheless let us go unto him." Thomas thought he meant that he was himself going to march now straight into the jaws of death and through them; so he said to the other disciples, "Come, let's go and die with him!" He was trying to make sense of that "nevertheless;" and it wouldn't make sense! There was another day when Jesus gathered up into his hands an immense and cosmic catastrophe: "There shall be signs in the sun, and in the moon, and in the stars; and upon the earth distress of nations with perplexity"; then added—as if to say "No matter! Never mind!"—"When these things begin to come to pass, look up, lift up your heads."

I wish you could have heard it from his lips, without the aid and comfort of these two thousand years that have followed. You should have had your chance too to sneer and turn away! Over and again he would set down his account of the human situation, yours or mine at its worst; reckon in every human resource, like a man getting ready for battle; pile up the terrible odds on that other side high enough to suit anybody's taste: then blithely wreck the whole business! "In the world ye shall have tribulation"—the very word means that you'll be put through the mills, ground fine as flour—"but be of good cheer". Then this studied, settled effrontery, this "humble, outrageous arrogance," there in the little room on that deadend street, the night before he was crucified: "I have overcome the world." You'll never get Christ's measure, you'll never know what the resurrection has to say about the obstacles which life tries to set in the middle of God's road, until you chart the distance in that utter about-face: this "Nevertheless" that God uttered the first day of the week, very early in the morning, as it began to dawn. Never will you understand what sense it makes until you see what nonsense it is: holding out to us the exhaustless mercy of God, in spite of what we are, because of what he is; with nothing now between him and us here but the coming of a child in a manger, and the death of a man on a hill!

So it is that the apostle gives answer: "He that spared not his own Son, but delivered him up for us all, how shall he not with him also freely give us all things?" You should make a careful note in these verses of those two words, "all things." "In all things—God!" "Freely—all things!" "In all things—more than conquerors!" He's saying it time after time after time, trying to persuade you of it, insisting that God means, soberly and honestly means, to make it worth your while to go on and go through, brushing the sweat off your face for his love's sake, wiping the tears from your eyes. You think he isn't up to it, will not bother with it? Look at the morning paper, you say: there you'll see how it is, while we're sitting here, tonight when we are asleep! And Paul keeps insisting that Christ will match it and more: the Christ who died hoping we would believe that, and rose again so that some day this faith might get into men's blood, and they would go out to meet the future as he did, with something in them that wouldn't be daunted and couldn't be beaten! Promising them, even as the shadows grew darker, that he would carry it off, whether they were there to see it or not; that if only they'd keep their muscles flexed and their nerves strung tight, they could afford to be defeated, as he could: because God wouldn't! It's too late for him to fail now, even with us!

I read a parable not long ago about a little lad who was walking through a dark forest holding the hand of his father. It was a pretty picture. The moonlight shone weirdly through the trees. In it every bush seemed to take on some bizarre and ghostly shape, stealing by, or creeping up, reaching out its arms, clutching with its fingers. There were roots and holes, and the child would stumble. Branches crackled, night birds called and flapped their wings overhead. But he held fast to the "strong and knowing hand of his father," and marched bravely on. I wish it were that easy. Nobody has a right to make it so!

It isn't, and never was. God had to do more than simply to pronounce this huge reversal of his, this infinite rebuttal, by which we are offered eternal life, we the dead,

GOD'S GREAT NEVERTHELESS

says Calvin; told of resurrection while surrounded by decay; called righteous, when sin dwells within us; hear that we are blessed, and with abundant goods, though we are rich only in hunger and thirst!

In Gethsemane and on Calvary Jesus wrenched his "Verily, verily, I say unto you" out of the world's hands. As it was trying to say, "No!" with its hammer and its nails, he broke through to the "Yes!" and won it—never mind the wild beasts in Pilate's court, howling for his blood! How else could it ever have been seared on men's hearts in such letters of fire? On what other terms would Peter have gone telling of his glory "a many hundred miles to Rome," or Paul "to the sharp sword outside the city gates, glad beyond words to drink of his sweet cup?" Jesus lived out and died clean through God's "Nevertheless." And there's more in it now than a lad's hand in his father's, swinging away through the dark woods!

There is in it now all the turning, twisting ingenuity of God's grace! Charles Peguy wrote of it once, how insidious it is, how full of surprises. "When it doesn't come from the right it comes from the left. When it doesn't come straight it comes bent, and when it doesn't come bent it comes broken. When it doesn't come from above it comes from below; and when it doesn't come from the center it comes from the circumference. . . . Certainly the modern world has done all it can to . . . rid itself of . . . every atom and trace of Christianity. But if I catch sight of something they can't conquer or submerge or comprehend, creeping out again from below, creeping in from the surroundings, creeping in from all around, am I to miss my chance of hailing it just because I was not up to calculating where it would come from? . . . This people will finish by a way they never began. This age . . . will get there along a road it never set out on." After that he died in the Battle of the Marne!

"What shall we say then to these things?" What things? It doesn't really matter in the New Testament! What shall we say to tribulation and distress? To life as it keeps closing in, so often with a "No Exit" sign where you thought there was a door? To God himself, waiting there at the end of the world, in the hour of death? Waiting here now in "holiness and judgment?" Trying the best he knows—in *us* to invade his world! From one of my classes comes the story of how it was when the allies landed on the beaches of Normandy. "Waiting in the stillness of dawn," ran the letter, "there was an oppressive silence. Eyes were straining at an angle above the water: the whine of landing craft pushing their burdens toward the shores of Europe, every man holding vigil at his station. Great expectancy was in the air. Here at last was D-day! We could look back at the blood and tears and the mighty planning which had brought it." Bethlehem in the gospel, and a cross! "And we looked forward to victory. On this razor's edge of time, our hearts beat with joy."

Can't we settle it now, how to answer back? "It is Christ that died, yea rather, that is risen again." As things pile up—and God moves in!

18

THE IMPACT OF THE RESURRECTION

by FREDERICK W. SCHROEDER

President, Eden Theological Seminary,
Webster Groves, Missouri

"And they went out and fled from the tomb; for trembling and astonishment had come upon them; and they said nothing to any one, for they were afraid."

—MARK 16:8

"But thanks be to God, who gives us the victory through our Lord Jesus Christ. Therefore, my beloved brethren, be steadfast, immovable, always abounding in the work of the Lord, knowing that in the Lord your labor is not in vain."

—I CORINTHIANS 15:57, 58

THE Easter event is beyond doubt at one and the same time the most baffling and the most dynamic event of all time. It is the most baffling because it is without precedent or parallel in human experience. Medical science has performed many miracles of prolonging life, but it has never restored a deceased person to life. People, seemingly dead, are known to have been resuscitated, but Jesus' triumph over death is a resurrection, not a resuscitation. As such it stands in a class all by itself, impervious to rational analysis or explanation.

Scientific investigation of the event is as impossible as it would be unproductive; neither is it likely that archeological discoveries will ever shed light on its historicity. Devout believers—not all, to be sure—as well as confirmed skeptics have intellectual difficulties with the resurrection. Many look for the kind of evidence that Thomas wanted when he said, "Unless I can put my fingers in the nailprints in his hand and my hand in the wound in his side, I will not believe." And not being able to come up with that kind of evidence they find the resurrection to be a stumblingblock to faith.

But strangely enough this stumblingblock to faith, if such it should be, is the very cornerstone of the Christian faith. Except for the resurrection the Christian movement would never have been born. Though the word of the Cross is commonly regarded to be the central theme of the gospel there simply would be no gospel if the Cross had been the last word.

But the Cross was not the last word. Easter followed Good Friday. And Easter, mystifying as it may be, turned defeat into victory. Its dynamic effect overshadows its baffling aspect. No other event has had such a powerful impact upon the course of human events as the resurrection. And while the impact of Easter may not resolve the mystery and miracle of the empty tomb, it confronts us with such an array of effects that the mystery ceases to be troublesome.

The passages of Scripture quoted above are only two of many that speak of the impact of the resurrection. Its immediate effect was, as Mark's account clearly indicates, fear and astonishment. Its long-range and more permanent effect was faith and steadfastness wherever the resurrection became a fully-apprehended reality.

Beyond this the New Testament bears witness to the impact of the resurrection in a variety of ways. In one of his letters Paul speaks of knowing Christ "and the power

THE IMPACT OF THE RESURRECTION

of his resurrection;" in another he testifies that "as Christ was raised from the dead by the glory of the Father, we too might walk in newness of life." And when Peter declares that "the stone which the builders rejected has become the head of the corner" he obviously had the resurrection in mind. But why multiply words when the facts of history speak far more convincingly?

Some of these facts are so well known that one need do no more than make them a part of the record. Consider, for instance, what Easter did for and to the disciples. Good Friday had left them a dejected, defeated company. Though Jesus had previously told them of his impending death and resurrection they admitted later that "they understood none of these things." Little wonder, then, that they were about to return to their former occupations. Then came their encounter with the risen Lord. Almost overnight these dull-minded, disillusioned, disheartened disciples became confident, courageous, persuasive apostles of the faith. Did this change come about by a gradual process of study and growth? Hardly! Only the impact of the resurrection accounts for a change so swift, so complete, and so dramatic.

Far more impressive is the beginning and the growth of that movement that we call the church. Except for the resurrection there would be no church. The church might well be called a monument of the resurrection; not a monument carved out of stone or wood or cast in bronze, but a monument throbbing with life wherever two or more gather in his name. Unheralded and unexpectedly, without the fanfare of publicity and promotion, this movement of the spirit came into being when the apostles proclaimed to an assembled multitude the mighty deeds of God in the life, death and resurrection of Jesus Christ.

The resurrection was and still remains the foundation

of the church. Under the impact of this event the church has withstood persecution from without and corruption from within, and has marched across the centuries with its continuity unbroken, its vision undimmed, its zeal undiminished, and its faith unshaken. Without a living Lord such a record is inconceivable. A martyred and dead prophet, however heroic his life and noble his teaching, would not today inspire and hold the loyalty of more than seven hundred million people in east and west, north and south. When one has intellectual difficulties with the resurrection—and some of us do now and then—it is good to think of the church. Its history, its motivation, its mission is a far more convincing witness of the resurrection than any argument of philosophy or any formula of science.

And the impact of the resurrection does not end with the life and work of the church. Consciously and otherwise the whole world has come to reckon with the importance of this event. Because of it Christ has become the midpoint of time. Strange, is it not, that one who lived in an obscure country of the Orient, who died the death of a criminal on a despised Cross should now be the one from whose birth all time is reckoned. Was this decided by some Gallup Poll of public opinion or by some majority vote of a world-wide ballot? No; this division of history into B.C. and A.D. must be regarded as the unpremeditated, unplanned impact of the resurrection, which introduced something so revolutionary and dynamic into history that human life and effort acquired a new direction and dimension. All this is written in letters so large that every one may read as he runs.

The resurrection invests life with worth and gives meaning to all human effort and activity. In the pre-resurrection era a wise man was moved to say: "Vanity of

THE IMPACT OF THE RESURRECTION

vanities! All is vanity. What does man gain by all the toil at which he toils under the sun?" Twentieth Century agnostics who deny the resurrection and materialists who in their pursuit of things ignore it, have a similar view of life. Whereas the agnostic builds his life on a philosophy of unyielding despair and may speak of man as "fear in a handful of dust" or as "a sick fly taking a dizzy ride on a gigantic fly-wheel" soon to be cast into the oblivion of nothingness, the materialist simply declares: "Eat, drink and be merry, for tomorrow you may die."

But when you look at life and man's activity from the perspective of the resurrection you get an entirely different slant. Then you are moved to say what Paul said at the conclusion of his ode on the resurrection: "Therefore, my beloved brethren, be steadfast, unmovable, always abounding in the work of the Lord, knowing that in the Lord your labor is not in vain." Somehow the resurrection gives worth and meaning to all honest, upright toil. It affirms that whatever of truth, of beauty and of goodness is put into life and work will abide.

But perhaps we are not so much concerned about what happens to our toil and labor as we are about what happens to us personally. Is it merely self-love, or perhaps even egotism, that makes the thought of annihilation so abhorrent? I think not. Since time immemorial man has asked the question: "If a man die, shall he live again?" He has turned to science for an answer, and has received nothing more than a forbidding silence by way of reply. He has turned to philosophy, and philosophy has said that there are potentialities in man so great that it seems irrational that man should be annihilated at the point of death. But beyond recognizing man's desire and capacity to be immortal philosophy has no answer. The only sure answer to man's age-old question comes from the empty tomb. The risen Lord gives us the assurance: "Because I live ye too shall live."

Perhaps it is this assurance, growing out of and supported by the resurrection, that accounts for the strange phenomenon of churches filled to overflowing on Easter Sunday. Why it is that people, including many who seldom rise above the biological level of existence, or who regard everything even faintly miraculous with incredulity, nevertheless go to church on this particular day? Is the Easter church attendance nothing more than a pious custom or a sanctified fashion parade?

Sometimes one is tempted to draw this conclusion, but perhaps there is more here than meets the eye. People do not need to go to church to show off their spring finery. Could it be that this phenomenon gives voice to a kind of inchoate awareness of what the resurrection means in terms of life's purpose and man's destiny? No one may presume to speak with finality on that score, but it is possible that the impact of the resurrection has penetrated deeper into man's consciousness than his ordinary way of life suggests. Obviously this is not true in every instance, but Easter does point up the fact that a divine purpose runs through all of life and history, and that ultimately this purpose leads to fulfillment.

In so doing it answers another question that keeps bobbing up from time to time. It is the question: What is the ultimate outcome of the historical process? What we want to know is whether history is simply the meaningless rise and fall of civilizations, whether mankind is caught in the web of some cyclical movement of birth and death that is without rhyme or reason, or whether the course of history does move toward some far-off divine event that will give meaning to all the sufferings and frustrations of this vale of tears. Not so many years ago when the course

THE IMPACT OF THE RESURRECTION

of history seemed to be moving forward and upward by a kind of inherent necessity such questions received but scant attention. But the notion that mankind finds itself on a heaven-bound escalator has been found to be illusory.

Today the whole process appears to be in reverse. The tragic character of our era has become apparent to all but the most obtuse. All of creation appears to be "groaning and travailing in pain," to use Paul's descriptive phrase. Is all this anguish and agony to be for nought?

Again we must say, the only reassuring answer comes from the empty tomb. The Lord who triumphed over death and the grave in Joseph's garden is also the Lord of history. His arm has not been shortened. His kingdom is a coming kingdom and an everlasting kingdom. This affirmation still leaves some questions unanswered as to how and when, but the ultimate outcome is assured. Because of his confidence in the ultimate victory of life over death, of righteousness over iniquity, of truth over falsehood, Paul was able to admonish the Corinthian Christians to be steadfast, immovable, always abounding in the work of the Lord.

What was true then is true today. The impact of the resurrection is by no means confined to Jerusalem and Judea of the first century; it has extended across the centuries and it is felt to this very day, even when it is not formally acknowledged or fully understood. The victory we celebrate on Easter Sunday gives meaning and purpose to all of life and to every human effort and enterprise. Well may we sound the trumpets and lift our voices in the swelling chorus: "The Lord is risen, the Lord is risen indeed."

19

FESTUS

by JOSEPH SITTLER, JR.

Professor, Federated Theological Faculty, University of Chicago, Chicago, Illinois

THE reality and power of the resurrection of Jesus Christ is not attested by only those verses in the New Testament which record it, or by St. Paul's specific teaching concerning it. Like specks of bright mica in rock it sparkles and flashes all through the record. That is why it is correct to say that the entire New Testament is a resurrection document.

Just as in our common conversations with one another something that just "slips out," as we say, may be more revealing than things we intended to say, so in the New Testament. There, from unexpected corners, and from the lips of strange and unlikely people, we get these little testimonial flashes. They are important because they are accidental, because the man isn't interested in Jesus or the resurrection at all! He's just babbling along, telling his story, doing a job—and out it comes!

Take Festus, for instance. But before we take him we have to find him! He isn't a very important man in the New Testament. He was a kind of minor cog in the complex administrative machinery that Rome was running in the provinces she ruled along the Mediterranean in the First Century. He gets into the story as a minor actor in the course of a narrative about a major one. The only reason anyone remembers Pontius Pilate is because a

FESTUS

Jewish prisoner, Jesus, one fateful day was hauled before him. The only reason Festus is remembered is that he once had to handle the case of another Jewish prisoner, Paul of Tarsus.

It happened like this (you can read the whole story in the Book of the Acts, Chapters 22 through 26):

Paul went to Jerusalem to bring offerings and gifts to the Christian community there, met with James and the elders of the group. Upon the advice of the local Christians, he "went into the temple" to signify that he—although resolute in his gospel that Christ was not for Jews alone but for the entire Gentile world—had the freedom to live in observance of the law.

There he ran into trouble; and that trouble got him shunted around from hearing to hearing, from official to official, and from court to court. "The Jews from Asia, who had seen him in the temple, stirred up all the crowd, and laid hands on him, crying out, 'Men of Israel, help! This is the man who is teaching men everywhere against the people (God's elect!) and the law (God's covenant!) and this place (God's holy temple!).'"

Paul was rescued from what certainly would have been death at the frenzied hands of a mob only by the arrival of a detail of soldiers from the barracks of the occupying Roman forces—"and when they saw the tribune and the soldiers, they stopped beating Paul." On the way to protective custody in the barracks Paul asked permission to address the mob, got it, and made a speech. He recounted his life before Damascus, the awful and magnificent moment of a "great light from heaven" that begot in him a forgiving, reconstituting, proclamatory flame whose name was Jesus Christ. He told of what that flaming light had done to and for and with his own career—revealing a Lord, bestowing an abounding life, and becoming con-

JOSEPH SITTLER, JR.

crete in a mission. "Depart, for I will send you far away to the Gentiles."

This was too much! That the God of Abraham, Isaac and Jacob could be so undiscriminating as to enfold in his love and purpose the "lawless" Gentiles was an assertion so wild that it begot wildness. More than forty "strictly bound ourselves by an oath to taste no food till we have killed Paul."

The only safe place for the prisoner was Caesarea, the fortress of the governor. Thence, under military escort, Paul was sent; and Felix the governor heard the case, waited for bribes that never came, left Paul in prison until the arrival of Porcius Festus, appointed by the king to succeed the reckless Felix.

Festus heard the case, too, didn't know what to do as between his Roman sense of justice—which told him that the case was no good and that the prisoner was innocent under Roman law—and the pressure from the Jews who were determined to secure Paul's death. And just then the troubled Festus got a break! King Agrippa arrived and provided a splendid opportunity to pass the buck! And here is where our text comes in—

> And as they [the King and Queen Bernice] stayed there many days, Festus laid Paul's case before the King, saying, 'there is a man here who was left in prison by Felix, and when I was at Jerusalem the Jewish high priests and elders presented their case against him, and asked for his conviction. I told them that it was not the Roman custom to give anybody up until the accused met his accusers face to face and had a chance to defend himself against their accusations. So they came back here with me and the next day without losing any time I took my

seat upon the bench and ordered the man [Paul] brought in. But when his accusers got up, they did not charge him with any such crimes as I had expected. Their differences with him were about their own religion and about a certain Jesus who had died but who Paul said was alive. I was at a loss as to how to investigate such matters . . .' "

(Acts 25:15-20 [Goodspeed])

There is color, movement, even a certain humor in this story of the combination of duty and bewilderment that beset Porcius Festus. We can reconstruct in imagination about the kind of fix he was in. A Roman official, first of all, with a job to do; and a characteristic Roman directness in getting it done. His report to his superior is in the best tradition of Roman colonial rule: clear, factual, consecutive. And breathing through it all a quiet pride in his Roman rational legacy. Get the facts, know the law, apply the law, get justice done with no nonsense. A man doing his duty.

But there is bewilderment, too. For when Festus had *got* the facts he knew he had gotten stuff that didn't slot neatly under the usual rubrics of public disorder, treason, incitement to riot, etc. Here was no clean-cut situation of the sort that Roman law, or any law for that matter, could make easy sense of. The substance of the public tumult that had gotten Paul under protective custody was a mad story about "a certain Jesus who had died but who Paul said was alive."

Such a statement, we can imagine Festus pondering, might possibly make sense in the religious backwaters of the strange and passionate Jewish culture whose former territory the Romans were now governing. For, after all, a lot of things seemed to make sense for the Jews that could only cause another man to shake his head. This kind of a statement might be an "intelligible proposition" (so we would put it) in the context of a religious history that ignored the rational ideas of cause and effect, force and freedom, challenge and response, natural resources and balance of trade, etc. It ignored these—and generated such bizarre ideas about history as to spin and preserve the meaning of its *own* history around the stories of Exodus and Sinai. A nation that had produced the deep national heartbeat of Isaiah's sonorous songs of deliverance, and engendered the late-remembered frenzy of the Maccabee family did not lend itself to easy calculation.

So Festus, with a flat let-us-Romans-have-no-nonsense summary of the whole business simply admits to his royal superior, "I was at a loss as to how to investigate such matters."

We still are! We are still inclined to believe that facts are facts, all alike—and that facts of faith can be established by the same methods that have been so serviceable in the establishment of other facts. So we persist in treating Easter—begetting fact as if it were one instance in a matrix of surrounding facts—and believe that we have served the faith well if we can make a strong case for it.

The New Testament doesn't do that. In that resurrection-document the fact is affirmed, to be sure, but it is a kind of affirmation which sends out all kinds of signals that this is no *Roman,* or *natural,* or *psychological* fact. It is always presented in such a way as to invite the beholder to reflect that in this instance fact and faith are correlated in a unique way.

We are always tempted to improve on that holy kind of care about godly fact. And the more massive the improvement the more we applaud the effort forgetting that even our Lord remarked with some asperity, "Neither will they believe if one rose from the dead." We forget that an ever so spectacular effort to establish this fact as simply in continuity with other facts, and by the same methods, would belie the character of faith and make it unnecessary!

There is no Christian faith apart from the victory of God in Jesus Christ. Resurrection is the sign and signal of that victory; and it is a victory of *God!* This is no confirmation of a slippery surmise about immortality, nor another psychical datum to be only added to our humane suspicion that man has dimensions of significance which transcend the rational. That "God hath raised him up" is not something that, once established apart from *God,* or the raised-up man, leads us confidently to go on and declare, "and I believe in the resurrection of the body" as a flat report of a verifiable truth. That faith is in the Creed as a statement of faith; and it's a statement of faith on the same level and of the same order as "I believe in God . . . and in Jesus Christ, His only Son, Our Lord."

Festus had at least the sensitivity to acknowledge and the candor to admit that he was stumped. Within the church on this Easter morning we are not as stumped as he was, or for the same reasons. The difference is *not* that we can of ourselves establish a fact that Festus couldn't; the difference is that we see as he could not what kind of "relationship to something historical" is required to become and be a Christian. *Our* kind of clarity focuses upon and intensifies the decision of faith; it doesn't eliminate it, or make it easier.

And that is why a traditional prayer of the church on Easter Day includes the petition, " . . . we humbly beseech thee that by *thy special grace preventing us . . .*"

20

TOO GREAT FOR THE GRAVE

by RALPH W. SOCKMAN
Pastor, Christ Church (Methodist), New York, New York

"Death could not hold him."
—ACTS 2:24 (Moffatt)

THE Easter news started in a garden. Three sorrowing women had slipped through the shadowy streets of early morning to pay their respects at the tomb of their beloved leader who had been crucified two days before. Finding the stone rolled away, they ran to tell Peter who came rushing to the grave and found it empty. Bewildered, Peter and the disciples departed.

But Mary stood at the sepulchre weeping. There appeared to her a Presence, which at first she did not recognize; but as she beheld him, she became convinced and cried, "Master."

That same evening two disciples were departing from Jerusalem by the Emmaus Road. They were in deep depression. Their leader had been put to death. Their enterprise had collapsed. As they walked along, a Presence drew near, and began to throw scriptural light on the events which had happened in Jerusalem. Their hearts became strangely warm. And as this mysterious Presence tarried with them for the breaking of bread, the record is that they recognized him as their risen Lord. The Easter drama of that first day had only a few scenes and only a few characters.

TOO GREAT FOR THE GRAVE

Six weeks passed. Such a period is a pretty fair time to test a false report. If the resurrection accounts had been mere ghost stories, they would probably have lost their exciting interest after six weeks. Furthermore, ghost stories beget fear rather than courage in those who believe them. But the reports of the resurrection had changed the frightened disciples into brave spokesmen. And on the day of Pentecost they were gathered to celebrate their Hebrew festival. Then something creative occurred. They became so endued with spiritual power that they were able to speak and think beyond themselves. The outsiders who heard them were amazed.

But Peter stood up and stirringly reminded the crowd of the ancient prophecies about God pouring out his spirit upon his people. This which they saw was a fulfillment of prophecy, brought to its climax by the crucifixion of Christ, "whom God both raised up, having loosed the pains of death, because it was not possible that he should be holden of it." Moffatt translates Peter's word in this plain simple sentence: "Death could not hold him."

Such is the conviction which crystallized from the reports of Easter and the events that followed. However hard it may be to explain the Easter accounts, the historical fact is that Christ had become more of a power in Jerusalem on Pentecost, six weeks after his death, than he was on Palm Sunday. The temple authorities could not hold him down. Pilate could not hold him. "Death could not hold him." This is the Easter assertion.

Death could not hold Jesus Christ, because his was a *mind* too great for the grave.

Some cynics think that only the ignorant believe in immortality. Dr. John Haynes Holmes lists among those who have believed that life persists beyond the grave such men as Socrates, Plato, Cicero, Seneca, Descartes, Spinoza,

Kant, Goethe, Eddington and Robert Millikan. We mention these not merely to remind ourselves that the best minds believe in immortality, but that such minds seem too great to die with the body.

The foundation of my belief in life immortal reaches further back than the resurrection of Christ. The belief in life beyond has persisted through all ages and is practically universal in all races. The Egyptians storing the tombs of their beloved with rich treasures for future enjoyment; the American Indians placing in their burial mounds their bows and arrows for use in the happy hunting grounds hereafter are examples of the pervasive conviction that death is not the end.

This belief involves the very integrity of the universe itself. The Creator has endowed us with the power to love, to evaluate, to hope. These powers are as integral to human nature as the hunger of the body or the air we breathe. Certainly the Creator who keeps faith with the cravings of our bodily instincts will not play false to the other half of our natures. Certainly the Creator who guides through the boundless sky the path of the migrating bird on its unerring flight has not planted in man a migrating instinct only to mislead him when he sets out for the larger home of his soul.

We are told that a human body undergoes a complete renovation of cell structure every seven years. Some of us, therefore, have had several bodies. Yet through all these changes our personal identity continues. Does it not then seem possible, even logical, that personality can survive the extreme bodily changes of the grave? As Sir Oliver Lodge was wont to say, smashing the organ is not equivalent to killing the organist. The soul of man can go on expressing itself through some instrument other than this earthly body.

TOO GREAT FOR THE GRAVE

It is this fact which Christ stressed and demonstrated. He said, "Life is more than meat." He set his followers looking at things invisible and eternal rather than on things seen and temporal. He showed that ideas and ideals, judgments and values are as real a part of life as flesh and blood. He so convinced such a powerful mind as Dean Inge of St. Paul's, London, that when the latter lost his little eleven-year-old daughter, he could control his tears with these confident words: "If we are right in claiming for our judgments of value an authority no less than we allow to our judgments of fact, which come to us through our senses, we may assert with confidence that the souls of the righteous are in the hand of God, and what is dear to him will never be plucked out of the land of living."

Jesus so lived and taught that he brought glimpses of the kingdom of heaven into the here and now. He said, "The kingdom of God is in your midst."

Have we not all enjoyed some snatches of eternal life? Have we not all had some experiences so engrossing that we become oblivious to time, and "one crowded hour of glorious life is worth an age without a name." And we exclaim, "Ah, this is heavenly," and we have those moments of rare insight and lofty feeling when, as the Scripture says, we taste "the powers of an age to come."

There is a quality of life which is independent of the quantity. And that quality which lifts us above the limitations of time and lessens the fear of death, which makes us feel the nearness of heaven and the nowness of eternity—that is what Christ imparts to those who cultivate his company.

When we live close to Christ in our experience here, with Peter we say of Christ, "Death could not hold him," because the mind—his and ours—is too great for the grave.

Secondly we can say that Christ revealed not only a mind but also a *character* too great for the grave.

Look at any great man. What is the most important feature about him? Not the strength or beauty of his body, not the brilliance of his mind, but the quality of his character. A man's body reaches its prime perhaps in his forties, his mind perhaps in his fifties. But the building of character persists through a whole lifetime. The exercise and discipline of youth; the struggle, disappointments and successes of maturity; the memories and tranquillity of age—these all go into the developing of character. Having spent three score years and more in the process, will the Creator then toss him to the void as rubbish? What infinite waste of work! What infidelity to the human spirit!

The Creator who would throw away his noblest human characters would be more wasteful than the most extravagant of governments and more cruel than the most heartless of fathers. But the government of this universe is not wasteful in the material realm. All energy is conserved somewhere. Even the flame of the candle which seems to go out has sent into space rays of light which go streaming on. Will the Creator who conserves the ray of light throw away the characters which have been achieved at such infinite pains? Our reasons revolt at the idea.

Beethoven composed music far beyond the capacity both of the instruments and techniques of his day. His music compelled the creation of better means of expression. His biographer said of Beethoven, "Born into the day of small things, he helped the day to expand by giving it creations beyond the scope of its available means of expression. So it was literally forced to improve these means and thus grow with them—a method much used by emancipators of humanity."

TOO GREAT FOR THE GRAVE

Similarly Christ composed music of living too great for these bodies and this material world. He put thoughts and love and character into men which called for a larger life in which to fulfill them. Then he said to his followers, "I go to prepare a place for you."

There is nothing in the logic of the universe's fidelity nor in the teachings of Christ to warrant the belief that eternal life is given to every one as a sort of universal insurance policy guaranteeing us against want and hardship. The teaching of the Bible is that eternal life is something that we "lay hold on." We enter the hereafter, as I see it, by way of a schoolroom rather than a courtroom. It is not a case of getting by God without a sentence to hell, as one might get by an earthly court and go scot free. Our heavenly Father, like our Lord, is a teacher. He extends the course. He gives us another chance. But he does not change the rules of life's school.

God is just to reward us, but the rewards have to be earned. God is just to punish us, but his punishments are purposive and purging. We go on from where we are in the course. And if we have not learned much of good in this life, we shall have to start the next life without much of good. If we have not learned to like what Jesus liked, we cannot enter very far into the joy of our Lord.

We may survive death and be defeated by it. We may wake up beyond the grave and wish we had not. We may reach the realm of the spirit and be as little able to appropriate it as a South Sea savage could appreciate the discussions of a convention of scientists. And to be where we do not fit—that is hell. We might go where Christ had prepared a place for us, and be as ill at ease as a night club roué amid the meditations of a religious retreat. And that would be hell. To be worldly where things are pure and true, to be filled with hate in a realm attuned to love—that would be hell.

Let us not torture ourselves with old pictures of hell as a place of unending punishment. God is love, and love chastens only to redeem. Hence, unending punishment can hardly be reconciled with the Father of our Lord Jesus Christ. But on the other hand, let us not fool ourselves into thinking that to get by the gate of death is the guarantee of eternal bliss. Emerson remarked that people clamor for immortality when they have not shown ability to use this life. And Doctor Samuel Johnson once looked back on a day when he had been peevish and fretful, and asked himself, "Is this the kind of life to which eternity is promised?"

In the gospel we see the character of the Christ who "brought life and immortality to light." He told us that in seeing him we are beholding the Father. Hence we know the character of the God we can trust and the kind of life which death cannot hold.

Thirdly, Christ demonstrated a *love* too great for the grave. Some people assume that it is a sign of selfishness to crave life beyond the grave. Not so, it is love that calls most loudly for continuing life.

Why has mankind through all ages and all cultures yearned for immortal life? Why have the noblest spirits been convinced in their highest moments that death is not the end but only a passing through the door? Why do you and I, faced by the piercing reality of a loved one's death, feel sure that the beloved spirit must go on, and that, by the same token, we too can be worthy of the after-life? The answer to all these questions is the same: it is *love* that creates the longing and carries the conviction that life is too great for the grave.

Faith, yes; hope, yes; but the greatest of the abiding

TOO GREAT FOR THE GRAVE

sources of assurance is love. It is love which knocks at the door of death and asks for an answer. We want to know whether those we love live on. We may be brave enough not to be deeply concerned about prolonging our own lives, but can we stand beside the grave of a beloved wife or beside a brave little boy fighting for life, and say immortality does not matter? No, it is love that cries out for life eternal.

Why do we want those we love to live on? Why do we want to live on with them? To serve them, to continue loving them, since there is no life without them? To give them greater happiness and a fuller life than they have had? To enrich life here and now, because if we knew definitely we would not lose them in death, we could take more time here to "grow in grace" with and towards those we love without the constant fear that one day there will be no tomorrow?

Since God is love and Christ craved comradeship, we can believe that there will be fellowship in the hereafter. I believe that we shall know our loved ones better in the spirit realm than here where we see through a glass darkly, and where we often are too hurried to look at them. And I believe that we shall have fellowship with many who in this world are fenced off by class and color and creed.

Love has eternity in its heart. Love is above the ravages of time. Love peoples the shore of the next world with those we "have loved long since and lost awhile," and after a time the company of those who await us yonder is larger than the circle of those we must leave here. Thus, as Paul said, "love never ends" in this world or the next.

21

THE POWER OF HIS RESURRECTION

by DWIGHT E. STEVENSON

Professor, College of the Bible, Lexington, Kentucky

"That I may know him and the power of his resurrection . . ."

—PHILIPPIANS 3:10

AND God said, "I am tired of sending messengers; I will go myself." So God came to earth to be with us. Outside of Scripture few men have stated the significance of this coming better than Peter Taylor Forsyth, the late British theologian:

> "It was God himself that came to us in Christ; it was nothing about God, even about his eternal essence or his excellent glory. It is God that is our salvation, and not the truth about God. And what Christ came to do was not to convince us even that God is love, but to be with us and in us as the loving God forever and ever. He came not to preach the living God but to be God our life; yes, not to preach even the loving God but to be the love that God forever is." [1]

What an audacious, breath-taking thing to say! Yet this is precisely what the Gospel does say. It is impossible to be indifferent to it. Either it is the most devilish lie ever

[1] *The Person and Place of Jesus Christ* (Boston: Pilgrim Press, 1909), p. 354.

THE POWER OF HIS RESURRECTION

concocted or it is the very splendor of God. We can say of the incarnation what Dorothy L. Sayers said of the resurrection: "Now, we may call [it] exhilarating or we may call it devastating; we may call it revelation or we may call it dull, then words have no meaning at all." [2]

Suppose it is all true! Then surely our deepest prayer will be like that of Paul: ". . . that I may know him and the power of his resurrection. . . ."

But how are we to know him? We should like to think that we can know him by reasoning and thinking alone. We could then get out our philosophy books—our Plato, our Spinoza, our Kant and Whitehead—and at the end of the philosophers' quest we should find him, the fulfillment of all philosophy. He would be the QED at the end of the mental equation.

It is not that easy. The wisest philosophers who have also come to know Christ understand that they cannot know him through their philosophy. Take, for example, that God-intoxicated man, Blaise Pascal. At his death in 1662 it was discovered that he carried on his person a worn piece of parchment sewed into his doublet. It was dated Nov. 23, 1654, and it recorded rather cryptically the central revelation of his life. It contained these words: ". . . the God of Abraham, the God of Isaac, the God of Jacob, *not of the philosophers and scholars.*" This is directly in line with the prayer of Jesus himself: "I thank thee, Father, Lord of heaven and earth, that thou hast hidden these things from the wise and understanding and revealed them to babes. . . ."

A clue to the meaning of Pascal's worn parchment is found in these words of his written near the end of his life. Christ is speaking: "Console thyself, thou wouldst not

[2] *Creed or Chaos* (New York: Harcourt, Brace, 1949), p. 7.

seek Me if thou hadst not found Me. I thought of thee in Mine agony; I have sweated such drops of blood for thee . . . Dost thou wish that it always cost Me the blood of My humanity, without thy shedding tears?" [3]

This is where the piercing truth comes through: There can be no knowledge of the living Christ that costs us nothing. We cannot know him without meeting him, and we cannot meet him unless we come out of hiding and confront him in person. We shall not know him through our wisdom, or our much learning. We shall not know him through our goodness. We shall not know him through national, racial or even ecclesiastical inheritance. We cannot know him *en masse,* lost in a crowd, cloaked in anonymity. We must come out of hiding, one by one, and confront him in our naked persons, not for what we have or what we know or what we have achieved, but for what we are. And then we can begin to know him.

In Christ we do not meet merely another moral hero, inspiring us; we meet God himself claiming us. And this produces a crisis. We find ourselves standing at a forking road with only two ways before us. Either we must give in to him, surrender to him, like Thomas who knelt before him after feeling his wounds, and say, "My Lord and my God!" Or we shall join the mob before Pilate in front of the judgment hall and with murder in our hearts we will shout, "Crucify him!" These are our only choices. We shall accept him as Lord or we shall slay him.

But where shall we meet him? There are only two places: in the church and in the Bible. Ordinarily we suppose that we come to know Christ first in the Bible. Luther said, "The Bible is the cradle in which Christ lies." Presumably, then, if we want to meet him we must go there. The words

[3] Francois Mauriac (ed.), *The Living Thoughts of Pascal* (New York: Longmans, Green and Company, 1940), p. 98.

of the Bible are not dead words, any more than the words my son writes to me in a letter are dead. They pulsate with his mind and heart; they ripple with his laughter. Through the words of the letter he comes to me and I go to him. The Bible can be like that. The pulse of its words can get into our blood and merge with our heartbeat and call us to the great verbs of faith: *come, follow, learn, love, go, teach.*

Nevertheless, if I expect to meet a living Christ in the Bible I cannot remain in my armchair reading and thinking about him. I must be ready for action. For example, I sit reading about the man who went up to the temple to offer a gift; but once at the altar he remembered that he was at odds with his brother. Right in the middle of the service, he got up from his knees, left the temple, sought his brother and made his peace. Then he returned to complete his offering.

When I read that, if I am going to understand the story at all, I must lay my Bible in my chair and go out to seek the brother from whom I am estranged. I must make my peace with him. Then a miraculous thing will happen. When my heart is knit with the heart of my estranged brother, when the bitterness has been dissolved in the acids of forgiveness, I shall find that the Christ whom I left at home in a book has followed me, and that he is there in my meeting with my brother. For "where two or three are gathered in my name, there am I in the midst of them."

That meeting, in kernel and essence, is the church. In the Bible I came face to face with the Christ of history; I knew him there as Master and Teacher, but not as Savior. Only when I met him in the church—in that community of faith and love between myself and my brother—only then did I know him as the risen and living Savior.

It can be like that. We can meet Christ first through the Bible and know him there as Master and Teacher; and then we can be driven out to our brothers until we find the living Christ through the Holy Spirit living in his church, and we come to know him as living Lord and Savior. Robert McAfee Brown has truly said, "Only one who stands in the position of having been forgiven by his faith in Christ is in a position to know truly who Christ is." [4]

For most of us, however, the order will be reversed. We will meet Christ first in the community of faith and love, and we will then go on to learn more about him through the Bible. Let me illustrate. During World War II Japanese soldiers on the Philippine island of Panay massacred eleven American Baptist missionaries, among them a couple who had served long years in Japan. This couple requested and got a half hour's reprieve for private prayer. Then they were killed.

When their twenty-year-old daughter in the states learned about it, she was overwhelmed with bitterness against the Japanese. She sank deep down into the mire of this bitterness for days, until she was suddenly jerked out of it by a thought! "I wonder what mother and father prayed about during that half hour?" No sooner had she asked the question than she knew the answer, for she knew her parents. Surely, they had prayed, "Forgive them, for they know not what they do." After this the daughter went immediately to the nearest prisoner of war camp where she gave herself in voluntary service. She did it unstintingly, and in complete forgiveness. The prisoners submitted to her kindness with mounting curiosity. Finally one of them spoke out for all: "Why do you do this?" "Because Japanese soldiers killed my mother and father," she answered.

[4] *P. T. Forsyth: Prophet for Today* (Philadelphia: Westminster Press, 1952), p. 73.

THE POWER OF HIS RESURRECTION

Then they talked among themselves. They could not understand such enemy-forgiving love.

Months wore on. The war ended. Near Osaka there lived a farmer, the disillusioned and defeated Mitsuo Fuchida, former captain of the Japanese navy. He was the man who had led the attack of the 359 planes that bombed Pearl Harbor. Fuchida learned that a shipload of prisoners was returning to Japan, repatriated at war's end; so he went to meet the ship, hoping to see some of his old friends among the prisoners. He found one, Uraga, who told him the mystifying story of the American girl who had come to serve them in the prison camp. Now the perplexity of the prisoners became Fuchida's perplexity. Writing of it later, he said, "I could not understand such enemy forgiving-love."

Shortly after this Fuchida had occasion to go to Tokyo. He took a train and emerged into Tokyo through the Sheybuya railway station. At the door he was handed a gospel tract which told the story of an American bombardier who had been taken prisoner by the Japanese and who had recovered his Christian perspective in prison by re-reading the Bible. When the war was over this ex-bombardier had returned to Japan to serve his former enemies as a missionary. Fuchida read the tract. More of the same, mysterious enemy-forgiving love! On impulse he went to a bookstore and bought a copy of the New Testament. He fell to reading the Gospel of Luke, and read it through until he came to the words of Jesus from the Cross, "Father, forgive them for they know not what they do,"

"Now I know," he said. "Now I know the secret of enemy-forgiving love." Then he did a dramatic thing. There on the streets of Tokyo near him stood a sound wagon. He strode to it, requested the use of the microphone, and to the startled passersby made this announcement: "This is Captain Mitsuo Fuchida speaking. I led the attack on Pearl Harbor. I want to tell you that I have become a Christian."

Where will you meet the living Christ? In the community of love and faith, where sin and forgiveness are real; and then in the living Bible. "Only one who stands in the position of having been forgiven by his faith in Christ is in a position to know truly who Christ is."

It is from this actual meeting with the living Christ that our doctrine of Christ is born. Said P. T. Forsyth: "We are to think about Christ whatever is required to explain the most certain thing in the soul's experience—namely, that he had given it the new life of God and mercy, and saved it from the old life of guilt, self and the world." I can know Christ as Lord when I have surrendered control of my life to him; and I can know him as Savior when I have experienced his forgiveness in the community of faith and love where he dwells.

I close with these classic words in the final paragraph of Albert Schweitzer's *Quest of the Historical Jesus*:

"He comes to us as One unknown without a name, as of old, by the lakeside, he came to those men who knew him not. He speaks to us the same words: 'Follow me!' And sets us to the tasks which he has to fulfill for our time. He commands. And to those who obey him, whether they be wise or simple, he will reveal himself in the toils, the conflicts, the sufferings which they shall pass through in his fellowship, and, as an ineffable mystery, they shall learn in their own experience who he is."

22

WHEN LIFE IS THE CLIMAX OF DEATH

by MORRIS WEE

Pastor, Bethel Lutheran Church, Madison, Wisconsin

I THINK there must have been some frenzied moments in hell during the tremendous hours when Jesus Christ was suffering and dying on Calvary's Cross. God was pitting his might against the powers of wickedness. Satan's claim upon the eternal souls of men was being contested by the Son of God. Darkness and desolation were being given their chance for conquest among the children of men. But evil and wickedness were defeated. Christ gained the victory that day and never again would despair and spiritual death be able to cover the souls of men of faith. When the Lord Jesus uttered his own committal service, "Father, into thy hands I commend my spirit," the battle was ended and victory achieved.

It must have been a triumphant day in heaven, with trumpets sounding as the conquering Christ mounted the bastions of eternity and walked between the welcoming hosts of angels and the redeemed to his high place at the throne of God. How the chants of praise must have rung!

The disciples of Jesus, on that first Good Friday, could not have guessed at the victory parade which the angels beheld. With them it had been only a cruel and bitter day. When Christ was crucified, it meant only heartbreak and shattered hopes, nothing more. They had seen their friend and master treacherously betrayed and unjustly condemned. They had felt the clutch of cold panic when the holiday crowd in an ugly mood had clamored for his death on a cross. They had hidden, afraid, and carried to their hiding places the fragments of their shattered dreams. Christ was dead. He was gone. Death had triumphed. The cunning of a jealous high priest and the influence of a cowardly governor had been enough to snuff out the life of their Lord as a candlelight is snuffed into nothingness. It had been so terrifyingly easy for Caiaphas and Pilate. They had smashed in one blow all that Jesus had seemed to be and mean. No wonder they hid. They could not face life bravely with Christ in a grave.

In the earliest flush of a Sunday morning, some women who had seen where the Lord was so hastily buried went to the cemetery to perform a last service of love for their dead friend. They would at least properly prepare his body for the long solemn sleep of the grave. They had no hopes. Their hearts were as heavy as the stone they had seen rolled before the grave entrance. They expected no one and wanted to see no one.

A stranger met them at Joseph's tomb, met them with a greeting which has transformed the whole world. It was an incredible thing he said. "Fear not. Ye seek Jesus of Nazareth. He is arisen, as he said. Come see the place where they laid him." "As he said." Of course he had said it many times but they had not understood it because they could not see how it could happen. After all, death was death, the end of life.

Then they saw him, talked with him, ate with him, walked the old familiar paths with him, met him at the familiar haunts on the shores of Galilee, heard his last instructions and felt the glow of assurance which accompanied his final benediction upon them. Jesus was alive. For him the grave was not the end of life. The climax of death was no ugly tomb but a new and radiant

WHEN LIFE IS THE CLIMAX OF DEATH

experience. Life, for Jesus Christ, became the climax of death.

The disciples became changed men, emerging from their scared retreats to speak boldly to those from whom they had hidden. Peter, who had been frightened by a servant girl's taunt, stood up to say, "We must speak of those things which we have seen and heard." The two friends from Emmaus, who had already put religion in the past tense, became vigorous crusaders for a risen Christ. The rest, afraid of the Jews before, came forward and "rejoiced to be counted worthy to suffer shame for his name." Their sorrows, fears and doubts were transformed by an electrifying confidence in God. They were no longer fearful. Rather, they were like people whose hearts hurt so much for sheer joy that they have no time to be afraid any more. Their personalities were warmed by an eternal flame lighted on Easter morning. On their lips was a great message. "Jesus Christ is risen. The first fruits of them who are asleep . . . Christ first, then they who are Christ's . . . Life is the climax of death."

Out into the world they went with that burning truth—only a gallant handful at first. But the rapture of their witness was so vivid and overpowering that it kindled the dying embers of the lost hopes of millions of others and so blazed into a great glory which can never be dimmed. Wherever this truth has gone, men's lives have been changed from grief and fear to joy and assurance. The Easter gospel is the world's triumphant message. Christ is risen! Life is the climax of death.

Well, what does it say in a world like ours? First, this: Christ, his church and his Gospel will never be defeated regardless of the apparently unfavorable odds. Without the Easter resurrection there would be no very hopeful prospects of that in this grim and hostile world. Indeed, then

Christ died on the Cross and that's the end of it with you and me underscoring the awful words he spoke, "My God, why hast thou forsaken me?" The best any of us could do would be to say, "This Christ was a good man whose idealistic fancies exceeded the realities of life and whose enthusiasm ran ahead of his judgment" and go about our business thinking it was splendid to have known about him.

Since Easter, however, and because of it, the outlook of Christ and his program is one of assured conquest. He and his plans are linked up to a divine power which controls the ultimate destiny of the world. Pilate, Herod and Caiaphas are gone, lying in nameless graves. But Christ is alive gaining a sustained and increasingly complete victory. Nowhere has an initial condemnation resulted in a more enduring triumph or greater vindication. So it is the glory of Easter to remind the world of the undefeated program of Jesus Christ. I think when we realize how many storms the church of Christ has lived through triumphantly, we begin to understand how great and strong it is. The old promise that the gates of hell shall not prevail against it holds firm.

In a world as antagonistic to the church as ours, we are tempted to be fearful of Christianity's chance of survival. But when we sense the throbbing power of the living Christ in it, we can face the hostile world and stare it down. We know that victory belongs to him who climaxed death with life. John Masefield has written a play about the crucifixion in which one of the characters tells Pilate's wife of Christ's death. The governor's wife asks, "Do you think he's dead?" When the answer is given, "No, lady, I don't," she asks, "Then where is he?" To which the man replies, "He's let loose in the world, lady, where neither Roman nor Jew can stop him." Let loose in the world and no one can stop him! We who are Christians are part of the one

WHEN LIFE IS THE CLIMAX OF DEATH

great kingdom that will never perish. It cannot die because Jesus Christ who is its heart is eternally alive.

Since Christ is alive, he is available to us for our daily problems. Not alone does he guarantee his church. He offers his power to his friends for the daily round. Since Easter, God has given Christians a new kind of personal power, an inner strength which comes from an awareness of being at peace with him. Into our confusion, he comes with integration and design. We know that God is interested and involved in our common tasks. We become strong beyond human strength. Paul's declaration, "I can do all things through Christ who strengthens me" was no idle boast but a statement of a fact which he had seen worked out in human experience. Other Christians have learned that the Lord's power is just as available to them as it was to Paul. Men and women who truly seek him are finding his life in them every day just as they have for nineteen hundred years.

Harry Lauder, the Scotsman, who sang his way into the hearts of people, lost his only son in World War I. While groping in the valley of the shadow of his son's death, he found power to face life bravely. When his friends asked for an explanation, he replied, "There were three ways open to me, despair, drink or Christ. I chose Christ."

Out of the Civil War came a song by Julia Ward Howe,

"I have seen him in the watchfires of a hundred circling camps,
They have builded him an altar in the evening dews and damps."

My soldier friends of World War II wrote me, "Christ is with us and how we need him." In Finland a national leader, speaking of his nation's travail said to me, "We couldn't do without him, now." Today, it is Christ who sustains the Christian living under persecution.

We all need his steadying company. It's good to have him as a living friend, for underneath the surface of life there's so much loneliness, bewilderment and grief. Life is hard at any time but in a world rushing headlong in a race with catastrophe we need him in the same almost desperate way the early disciples did. Men and women in touch with the risen Christ can best be brave these days. They, like others, are perplexed but they have help. It has been available to all ever since life became the climax of death.

Christ is alive. It means that we shall outlast the stars. The dread of death is a common heritage. The hope of life after death is one of the most deepseated of human longings. All people yearn for a prophetic and sure word. It was Socrates who said, "I think I see the isles of the blessed. But, oh for a stronger ship to bear the way." Even the modern skeptic yearns no less, hoping, as one brave agnostic said of himself, hoping to hear the rustle of an angel's wing. But hopes and guesses, poetry and philosophy are barren and insecure to a faltering human being who stands beside a grave. They bring no comfort or peace, and make more inexplicable the meaning and mystery of death. Since Christ rose from the tomb, men have had a final and adequate answer. Life is the climax of death. The tomb which could not hold the Lord cannot hold those who share his eternal life. Death, on Easter morning, was swallowed up in victory!

In the first century of the Christian era a Roman general wrote a report on his progress in putting Christians to death. "These foolish people," he wrote, "think they are immortal. They go to their death as to a triumph and no threat of punishment has any effect on them." Eighteen hundred years later a Christian missionary captured by Communists and facing certain death wrote a letter to a friend and included a poem containing her thoughts on her anticipated martyrdom.

"Afraid of death? Afraid? Of what?
Afraid to see the Saviour's face—
to hear His welcome and to trace
the glory gleam from wounds of grace?
Afraid? Of that?"

And what was it Florence Buckner wrote?

"If death is to enter a city
And be hailed as a child of its King,
O grave, where soundeth thy triumph;
O death, where hideth thy sting?"

Across the centuries, apparently, there have been those who have known that because of Christ they will live long after every star has been pulled from its socket, that when the mountains are no more and rivers have stopped running into the sea, they will be alive and with Christ.

And with their loved ones. For they, too, shall outlive the stars—the dear ones to whom we have said farewell and over whose open graves the words have been spoken, "Blessed be the God and Father of our Lord Jesus Christ who according to his abundant mercy has begotten us again into a living hope by the resurrection of Jesus Christ from the dead."

In Christ, they too are alive and we shall yet see them.
"And so to me there is no death,
It is but crossing with abated breath
A narrow strip of sea,
To find our loved ones on the shore,
More bright, more beautiful than before."

It is Easter. Christ is risen. Life is the climax of death.